LEVEL E

Nila Banton Smith

Be a Better Reader

BASIC SKILLS EDITION

ADVISORY BOARD

H. Alan Robinson
Professor of Reading
Hofstra University
Hempstead, New York

Millard Black
Formerly Administrative Coordinator
Instructional Materials Center
Los Angeles Unified School District
Los Angeles, California

Mary Anne Burns
Secondary Reading Consultant
Kalamazoo Public Schools
Kalamazoo, Michigan

Frederick V. Davis
Coordinator of Reading
Board of Education
Elizabeth, New Jersey

Roselmina Indrisano
Associate Professor of Reading
Boston University School of Education
Boston, Massachusetts

Carolyn L. Lithgo
Language Arts Coordinator
Greensboro Public Schools
Greensboro, North Carolina

David E. Massey
Director of Language Arts
Hall County Schools
Gainesville, Georgia

Marilyn Moore
Reading Specialist
Shawnee Mission Schools
Shawnee Mission, Kansas

Bobbie Dean Shaw
Reading Specialist
Meridian Public Schools
Meridian, Mississippi

Prentice-Hall, Inc., Englewood Cliffs, N. J.

PRONUNCIATION KEY

Symbol	Key Word	Symbol	Key Word	Symbol	Key Word
a	act, lap	u	up, nut	n	nap, noon
ā	age, late	ū	use, few	p	play, top
ã	dare, hair	ũ	fur, learn	r	ran, steer
ä	star, father	ə	a in along	s	sit, yes
e	end, met		e in moment	t	tip, hat
ē	see, even		i in modify	v	very, wave
ê	here, clear		o in protect	w	wide, always
ẽ	over, under		u in circus	y	yellow, onion
i	hit, is	b	big, job	z	zebra, freeze
ī	ice, mile	d	do, red	ch	chill, reach
o	dot, plot	f	fair, if	sh	sharp, crash
ō	no, open	g	go, dig	th	three, both
ô	corn, border	h	head, behave	ŦH	then, breathe
oo	book, put	j	joke, bridge	zh	treasure
ōō	move, school	k	king, kick	ŋ	bring, think
oi	foil, boy	l	light, bell	'	heavy accent (stress)
ou	out, crowd	m	meet, him	'	light accent (stress)

Be a Better Reader, Level E, Basic Skills Edition
Nila Banton Smith

©1978, 1969, 1963, 1958 by Prentice-Hall, Inc., Englewood Cliffs, N. J. 07632

Printed in the United States of America

10 9 8 7 6 5 4 3

ISBN 0-13-074633-9

Prentice-Hall International, Inc.
London

Prentice-Hall of Australia, Pty. Ltd.
Sydney

Prentice-Hall of Canada, Ltd.
Toronto

Prentice-Hall of India Private Ltd.,
New Delhi

Prentice-Hall of Japan, Inc.
Tokyo

Prentice-Hall of Southeast Asia Pte. Ltd.
Singapore

Whitehall Books Limited
Wellington, New Zealand

Designed by Madeline Bastis & Friends

Art Credits:

Sal Murdocca: pages 7, 12, 16, 17, 18, 20, 24, 29, 30, 31, 52, 56, 68, 70, 75, 76, 78, 93, 107, 115, 121, 131, 139, 140, 142, 151, 161, 166, 179, 182, 183, 184, 187, 193, 200, 201, 203, 204.

Allen Davis: pages 5, 37, 38, 46, 47, 59, 72, 83, 85, 97, 105, 129, 171, 173, 191.

Don + Ann Crews: pages 13, 15, 32, 33, 43, 53, 54, 120, 135, 138, 144, 159, 177.

John A. Lind: pages 48, 49, 50, 95, 96, 109, 116, 119, 141, 143, 181, 182, 198, 199.

Photograph Credits:

pages 2 – Myron Wood/Photo Researchers; 3 – Mimi Forsyth/Monkmeyer; 8 – Culver Pictures; 10 – left: Culver Pictures; right: Wide World Photos; 14 – Wide World Photos; 15 – Ann Zane Shanks/Photo Researchers; 22, 25 – Wide World Photos; 40 – Rue/Monkmeyer; 42 – Wide World Photos; 43 – Pro Pix; 45 – left: Culver Pictures; right: Wide World Photos; 50 – Leonard Lee Rue III/National Audubon Society; 51 – Frederic Lewis ; 62 – Mimi Forsyth/Monkmeyer; 64 – Mahon/Monkmeyer; 65 – David Strickler/Monkmeyer; 66 – Mimi Forsyth/Monkmeyer; 73 – Wide World Photos; 80 – Culver Pictures; 82 – Todd Webb/Photo Researchers; 88, 89 – Culver Pictures; 90, 91 – Wide World Photos; 99 – Culver Pictures; 103 – Bill Anderson/Monkmeyer; 110 – top row left: Chris Bonington/Daily Telegraph Magazine; top row right: Pro Pix/Monkmeyer; bottom: Pro Pix/Monkmeyer; 111 – Perry Holzgraf/Monkmeyer; 112 – NASA; 114 – left: United States Navy; right: Wide World Photo; 126 – AT & T Photo Center; 126 – Mimi Forsyth/Monkmeyer; 132, 134, 135 – Culver Pictures; 136, 137 – AT & T Photo Center; 148 – Mahon/Monkmeyer; 149 – Sybil Shackman/Monkmeyer; 151 – Eliot Erwitt/Magnum; 152 – Erich Hartmann/Magnum; 154, 156 – Wide World Photos; 160 – Culver Pictures; 164 – Wide World Photos; 165 – Pat Morin/Monkmeyer; 169 – SUVA/DPI; 172 – Phil Carol/Monkmeyer; 176 – Wide World Photos; 178 – R. Redden/Animals, Animals; 181 – Jean-Paul Jallot/Photo Researchers; 191 – Wide World Photos; 195 – Syd Greenberg/DPI.

TABLE OF CONTENTS

Acknowledgments

[1]Adapted from C.F. Talman, "A Valley of Death and Prosperity." *The Mentor* Vol. 12, No. 6, p. 55.

[2]Adapted from *Pioneers and Patriots: The Lives of 6 Negroes of the Revolutionary Era* by Lavinia Dobler and Edgar A. Toppin, New York, N. Y., Doubleday & Company, Inc. ©1965.

[3]Adapted from an article in *Compton's Encyclopedia*, 1970 edition, F.E. Compton Company, Division of Encyclopedia Britannica, Inc., Chicago, Ill.

[4]Reprinted from the index, *Compton's Encyclopedia*, 1970 edition, F.E. Compton Company, Division of Encyclopedia Britannica, Inc., Chicago, Ill.

1

The Air Age

There are probably as many different reasons for reading stories as there are readers. Some readers may want to learn how other people live and how they solve their problems. Others may read to escape from their own problems. Still others may read to find adventures and experiences they will never have themselves. Although many readers may share some of these reasons with others, the combination of reasons is different for each person.

Kinds of Stories

Think about the kinds of stories you like to read — adventure, mystery, romance, true-to-life, fantasy. Do you like stories about people or about animals? Do you like stories that are set in strange, faraway places or in places like the one where you live? Once you know what kinds of stories you like, think about why you like them. Is it for escape, for adventure, for learning, or for some other reason or combination of reasons?

Enjoying Stories More

Whatever kinds of stories you like and whatever your reasons for liking them, knowing more about how stories are written will increase your enjoyment of them. All stories include these elements:

1. *plot* — the events or actions that happen in the story
2. *characters* — the people who are in the story
3. *conflict* — the struggle or problem that the characters face
4. *setting* — the time and the place where the story happens
5. *theme* — the main idea or meaning of the story

In every story you read, you will find the parts put together in a slightly different way. In one story, the people, or characters, may seem more important than the plot, and in another story, setting may be stressed. But all the parts are there — working together to make a story for you to enjoy.

More About Characters

One of the most interesting things about stories is the people who are in them — the characters of the story. Characters may be people who really lived, people the author has made up, or even animals. Sometimes authors even use a combination of these kinds of characters. For example, you may come across a story in which George Washington — a person who really lived — is in a situation with characters that the author has made up.

As you read the next story, pay special attention to the character and think about these questions:

1. Is the main character strong or weak?
2. What is the main character's most outstanding feature?
3. How does the main character act in difficult situations?
4. Do you think you would like to know the main character?

Working with New Words

Reading a story is always more fun if you don't have to stop and think about new words that you may not know. Before you read each story in this book, take time to look at the new words at the bottom of the first page. Study the pronunciation and the meaning, so the words won't be strange to you when you read the story.

Can you imagine flying alone in a small plane—and coast to coast at that? In the story that follows, you will read about an early flyer who did just that. Take right off and follow his adventures and hardships.

Nineteen Wrecks to Glory _____

Written for this book
by Glenn Munson.

Cal Rodgers was a big man—6 feet 4 inches (1.9 meters) and 200 pounds (90 kilograms) Square-jawed and handsome, he prided himself on his physical endurance.

He was also shy in crowds and now, as Chicago reporters backed him against the lower wing of his Wright Model B biplane, he clamped a fresh cigar between his teeth and puffed a protective cloud between himself and the reporters.

"Do you still think you can win the $50,000 from Mr. Hearst?" asked one reporter.

"The prize seems out of the question now," answered the flyer. "But I'm going to do this whether I get five thousand dollars or fifty cents or nothing. I am bound for the Pacific Ocean; and if canvas, steel, and wire, together with a little brawn, tendon, and brain stick with me, I mean to get there."

Then, as if to prove his point, Cal jumped onto the lower wing and climbed into the cockpit. Settling himself on the hard, flat seat, he lowered his goggles and nodded to the mechanics waiting at the twin propellers mounted behind the wings. A moment later Cal Rodgers' *Vin Fiz*, its small engine whining at full speed, bounced across the turf of Chicago's Grant Park, then lifted into the air amid the cheers of thousands of spectators.

*   *   *

When, in late 1910, William Randolph Hearst had offered $50,000 to the first person to cross the continent by air, he had made two rules. The prize was offered for one year only, and the flight had to be completed in 30 days or less.

By the fall of 1911, several people had announced plans to seek the prize; but most of them had never taken off, and the rest had quit after short distances. Said Cal Rodgers, "Someone had to do this flying, and I decided I might as well be the one."

By September Cal was ready to go, sponsored by the makers of a new grape drink called Vin Fiz. Both his biplane and the hangar car of the special three-car train that would follow Rodgers to California were painted white with large purple letters spelling "Vin Fiz."

A large crowd gathered at the racetrack in Sheepshead Bay on a warm, sunny September day to see Rodgers off. After a young woman christened the biplane by pouring a bottle of grape drink on it, Cal lit a cigar, waved, and took off, headed for California.

---

biplane (bī′plān′), an airplane with two wings, one above the other.

demolished (di mol′ishd), destroyed, ruined.

tumultuous (tōō mul′chōō əs), noisy and violent.

turbulent (tūr′bū lənt), disturbed, rough.

shards (shärdz), broken pieces of pottery, glass, or metal.

strut (strut), a brace fitted into the framework of a plane to strengthen it.

After circling Coney Island dropping Vin Fiz leaflets, Cal skimmed Brooklyn at 800 feet, then flew across Manhattan. "Thousands of persons witnessed the most inspiring sight of their lives when Rodgers sailed across the city," wrote one New York newspaper.

Over New Jersey, Cal spotted the special train that carried enough spare parts to build another plane. The train also carried an automobile; Cal's wife, mother, and cousin; and a few mechanics, including Charley Taylor, the Wright brothers' chief mechanic.

Rodgers followed the train north to Middletown, where nine thousand people awaited him at the fairgrounds. "I came down so easily," Cal wrote in his diary, "it didn't knock the ashes off my cigar. It's Chicago in four days if everything goes right."

It didn't. Trouble began early the next morning. On takeoff, the wheels snagged in a willow tree, flipping the biplane over. It landed on a chicken coop in a tangle of wire, wood, canvas, and feathers. Head bleeding, Rodgers was still puffing the cigar he had lit just before takeoff, but his gleaming Vin Fiz was demolished.

Three days later the rebuilt Vin Fiz covered 95 miles (152 kilometers) in one afternoon. "I was above the air currents going faster than the wind," wrote Cal. "The engine went on singing a sweet song. I lit a fresh cigar and let her go."

The next day a defective spark plug popped out of Cal's engine. Then the Vin Fiz was demolished for the second time three days later, when it ran into a barbed-wire fence. But the mechanics worked around the clock and a few days later Cal flew into Ohio, having covered a record 204 miles (326 kilometers) in one day. "Sailing above Akron was as enjoyable as any day I have had," Cal wrote. "I could light cigars with ease at any stage of my flight. Let's hope the rest of the trip is as smooth as today was."

Crossing into Indiana, Cal got caught up in a thunderstorm. No one had ever flown in a storm like that and lived to tell about it.

"I knew the turbulent air would tear the plane apart," he wrote, "so I swung her and streaked east only to run bang up against another big rain cloud. If you have been out in a hailstorm you know how that rain cut my face. It was bad. I could have been a million miles up in space. I could have been a hundred feet from earth. I couldn't see a thing."

Three weeks after leaving New York, Rodgers landed in Chicago. He had flown only 1,000 miles (1,600 kilometers) during his twenty-three and a half hours in the air and had lost his chance at the Hearst prize. But he was not going to quit, as the others had. "I am going to keep going simply to be the first to cross this continent in an airplane," Cal said.

Three days later he flew into Kansas City, where schools were let out so that children could see him and the famous *Vin Fiz.* A week later he landed at the Texas State Fair, in Dallas, "amid tumultuous applause from an eager crowd of 75,000 persons," said a Dallas paper.

On October 25, flying west of Austin, the *Vin Fiz* was again demolished when the right propeller struck the ground on takeoff. Cal said, "These wrecks are part of the game and are to be expected. Of course they are unwelcome."

On November 3, Cal's engine exploded near the Salton Sea, California, driving metal shards into his right arm. He glided down for a perfect landing, and it took a doctor over two hours to remove the slivers of engine from Cal's arm.

Two days later the *Vin Fiz* reached Pasadena. Cal had been traveling 49 days. He had covered 4,230 railroad miles in three days, ten hours, and four minutes of

actual flying time. He had had 19 crashes— four of them requiring a complete rebuilding of his plane. Only the rudder and one strut remained of the original biplane.

Landing in Tournament Park, Rodgers was mobbed by twenty thousand wildly cheering people. Police had to clear a path for him. Cal was given an American flag, paraded around the field in an open car, then taken to a hotel, where he celebrated by drinking a glass of milk and eating crackers.

The country went wild, hailing Rodgers' heroic feat, but Cal did not consider his trip over yet. A week later he left Pasadena for Long Beach and the Pacific Ocean. Halfway there he crashed during an emergency landing—his *Vin Fiz* demolished for the fifth time.

Pulled from the wreckage unconscious, with a broken ankle and many bruises, Cal did not revive until the next day. Smoking a cigar and talking with friends, Cal said he didn't know what had caused this crash. "Anyway," he went on, "I know I hit the ground a mighty hard whack. But it's all in the ball game. I am going to finish that flight and finish it with the *Vin Fiz.*"

On Sunday, December 10, Cal hobbled across a field and climbed aboard the rebuilt *Vin Fiz,* tucking his crutches behind him. Taking off for Long Beach, he landed there in the sand and wet his wheels in the Pacific Ocean as a crowd of 50 thousand people cheered. His historic flight was finally over.

And so, nearly, was his life. On April 2, 1912, Cal took off for a short flight around Long Beach. While flying out over the water a few yards from the beach, his plane hit a flock of seagulls and plunged out of control into the ocean. He was immediately pulled from the wreckage by swimmers, but it was too late. His neck was broken. He died a few feet from the spot where he had made history only four months earlier.

ACTIVITY 1 Fact Questions

On your paper, write the answers to these questions.

1. When did Hearst make his year-long prize offer?

2. What was the time limit for the flight?

3. Was Rodgers the only person trying for the prize?

4. What kind of plane did Rodgers fly?

5. Why was his plane called the *Vin Fiz*?

6. Where did Rodgers start his flight?

7. Who and what rode the special train?

8. How long did it take Rodgers to reach Chicago?

9. How many days did it take him to reach Pasadena?

10. How did Cal finally end his historic flight?

ACTIVITY 2 Thought Questions

Write the answers to these questions. Use your own paper for your answers.

1. Why do you think Cal Rodgers wanted to fly across the country in a little biplane under dangerous conditions?

2. What does the story tell you about Cal's character?

3. What personal character trait do you think was most important for Cal's flight?

4. Cal Rodgers set out to win the Hearst prize. Would you say his flight was successful?

5. Do you think he was foolish to keep going once the prize was lost and he had so many difficulties and accidents?

6. How did Cal's diary indicate his philosophy toward life and his risky flying venture?

ACTIVITY 3 Thinking About Characters

As you read the story, you were thinking about the four questions asked on page 3. Now that you have read the story, look back at those questions. Write the answers to them on your own paper.

**HOW TO READ IN
SOCIAL STUDIES**

The selection that follows is much like the material that you find in your social studies or history books. As you go on in this book, you will find more selections like these, and each time you will learn more about how to read this kind of material to get the most out of it. You will also learn how to use the aids that sometimes are used with such material.

In much social studies material, you will find headings that tell you what a paragraph or group of paragraphs is about. You will find it helpful to read these headings first to get an idea of the material covered before reading the whole selection. Follow these steps in reading the selection that follows:

1. Read all the headings. Think about what each one means and what will be discussed under it.
2. Do Activity 1.
3. Read the entire article carefully. Pay special attention to the order in which major events happen.
4. Do Activities 2 and 3.

Today, we think nothing of stepping onto a huge jet with hundreds of other passengers and arriving five hours later on the other coast of the country. But it wasn't always so. Less than a hundred years ago, there weren't even any planes. Read the following selection to discover how far we've gone in the air—and beyond.

The Development of Aircraft _____

The First Airplane Flights

People have always wanted to fly. Even in ancient times, attempts were made to travel through the air, but such attempts ended in failure.

At last, balloons were invented that made successful flights. Later, a great deal of interest developed in the use of gliders without engines. Then came the airplane with a gasoline motor.

The first successful airplane flights were made by Orville and Wilbur Wright in 1903, at Kitty Hawk, North Carolina. Orville made the first flight and stayed in the air twelve seconds. Wilbur made the next flight and stayed in the air almost a minute. The Wright brothers, who repaired bicycles, had made their plane from odds and ends in their workshop. It wasn't until 1908, after they had shown their plane in Europe, that other Americans paid attention to their invention.

---

development (di vel′əp mənt), gradual unfolding.

Blériot (blār′i ō), a famous aviator.

feat (fēt), a notable act or performance displaying skill or daring.

That same year Glenn Curtis made a flight, remaining in the air long enough to travel one mile. After that, one person after another made an attempt, each setting a new record of both speed and distance. In 1909 Louis Blériot, a Frenchman, flew from France to England.

World War I Spurs Interest in Airplanes

Experimenting by inventors might have gone on for years with slow progress had it not been for World War I, 1914 to 1918. When the first plane flew over European battlefields, people throughout the world began to think of uses to which the airplane might be put, both in wartime and in peace. Many countries tried to improve their airplanes. As a result it was a time of great progress.

Travel and Industry Hasten Airplane Development

In 1927 Charles A. Lindbergh, a young airmail pilot, thrilled the world by flying from New York to Paris in 33 hours and 31

minutes. Businesses began to recognize the value of air travel when they saw that trips that had taken weeks could be made in days or hours. People began traveling by airplane instead of by train or steamship. Farmers found they could ship foodstuffs great distances very quickly. Industries, too, discovered that airplanes could carry their products from factory to markets both quickly and safely. Even postal service could be speeded up.

The increasing demand for these new services led to a great growth of the airplane industry. New designs for larger, safer, and faster planes were developed. New landing fields appeared. Runways were enlarged. Pilots had to be hired to fly the planes. Many other people were needed to work in new industries which came into being with the manufacturing of airplanes.

New Developments During World War II

During World War II, 1939 to 1945, the airplane became very important in warfare. Many new planes were developed to serve different purposes: transport planes, fighter planes, bombers. Jet fighters with speeds of over 600 miles (960 kilometers) per hour were developed during this period. These new planes came as a result of World War II.

Present Struggle for Speed and Distance

Since the close of World War II, the capability of jets has been much increased. Jets are replacing older kinds of airplanes for many purposes in travel and industry. Faster jets—called SST's, for Supersonic Transport—have been developed. The first passenger flights of SST's between Europe and the United States began in 1976.

In spite of all these developments in airplanes, however, we are not yet satisfied. We want to go faster and farther. This fact accounts for the strong interest at present in improving rockets. Invented by Professor Goddard in 1926, modern rockets are extending our reach millions of miles into space. With rockets, we are learning more and more secrets of the universe. This knowledge may someday make it possible for you, yourself, to look upon wonders that no one before you has seen.

ACTIVITY 1

Summing up Headings

The headings in this article sum up the five important periods in airplane development. Number your paper from 1 to 5. Then write in order the names for the five periods. You may use your own words, but do not look back at the article.

ACTIVITY 2

Using Time Lines

Study this time line; then answer the questions. Write the answers on your own paper.

1. Which happened closer together?
   a. The Wrights' flight at Kitty Hawk and Blériot's flight to England.
   b. Blériot's flight and the beginning of World War I.

2. Lindbergh's flight was farther from
   a. the end of World War I.
   b. the beginning of World War II.

3. Give the date for each of these events:
   a. U.S. astronauts landed on the moon
   b. The flight at Kitty Hawk
   c. Passenger SST flights to the U.S.
   d. The invention of the rocket

4. How many years passed from the launching of the first satellite to the landing of a spacecraft on Mars?

The Development of Aircraft

1900	
1903	Wright brothers made first flight at Kitty Hawk
1908	Curtis flew one mile
1909	Blériot flew across English Channel
1910	
1914–1918	World War I. Improvements made on aircraft
1920	
1926	Goddard invented liquid fuel rocket
1927	Lindbergh flew from New York to Paris
1930	
1939–1945	World War II. Many improvements made on aircraft
1940	
1949	Army two-stage rocket reached 250 mile (400 kilometer) height
1950	
1954	Navy single-stage rocket reached 158 mile (253 kilometer) height
1957	Russians launched first satellite
1958	U.S. launched its first satellite
1960	
1961	Russians put man into orbit U.S. launched manned space flight
1962	U.S. put man in orbit
1966	Surveyor I landed on the moon and sent pictures back to the U.S.
1969	U.S. astronauts landed on moon
1970	
1971	Mariner IX orbited Mars
1973	U.S. spacecraft flew by Jupiter
1975	U.S. and Russia in first joint space mission (Apollo-Soyuz)
1976	Viking landed on Mars
1976	SST passenger service to U.S. is begun.
1980	

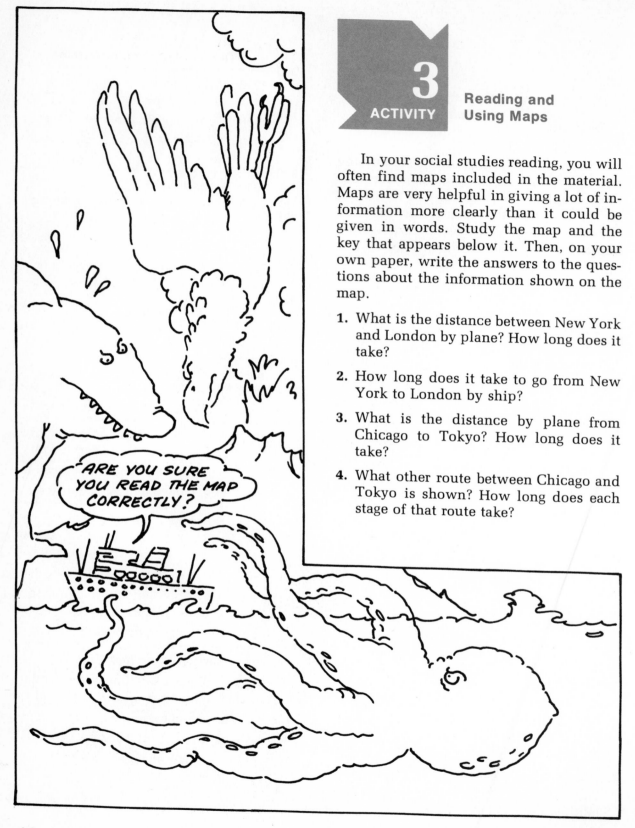

ACTIVITY

Reading and Using Maps

In your social studies reading, you will often find maps included in the material. Maps are very helpful in giving a lot of information more clearly than it could be given in words. Study the map and the key that appears below it. Then, on your own paper, write the answers to the questions about the information shown on the map.

1. What is the distance between New York and London by plane? How long does it take?

2. How long does it take to go from New York to London by ship?

3. What is the distance by plane from Chicago to Tokyo? How long does it take?

4. What other route between Chicago and Tokyo is shown? How long does each stage of that route take?

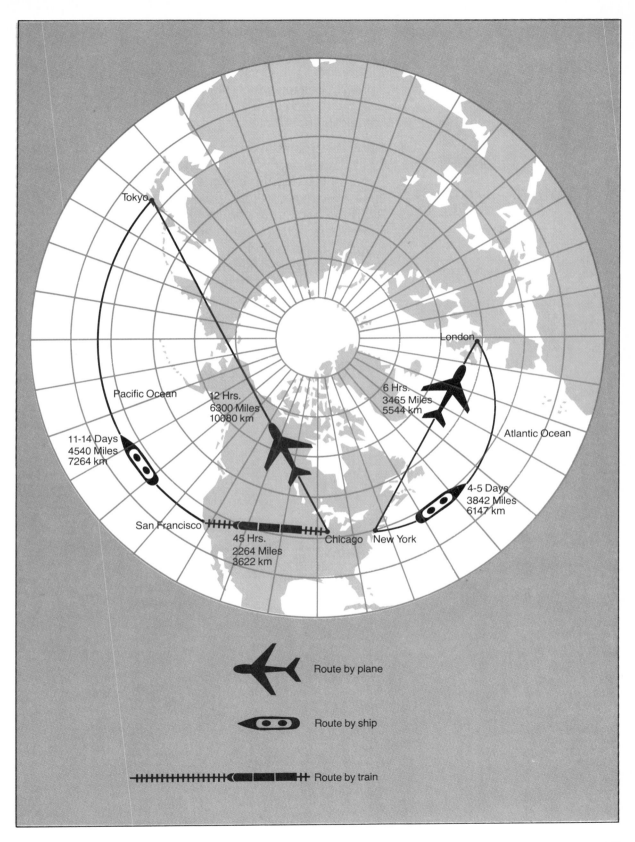

Tokyo

Pacific Ocean

12 Hrs.
6300 Miles
10080 km

London

6 Hrs.
3465 Miles
5544 km

Atlantic Ocean

11-14 Days
4540 Miles
7264 km

4-5 Days
3842 Miles
6147 km

San Francisco

45 Hrs.
2264 Miles
3622 km

Chicago   New York

Route by plane

Route by ship

Route by train

HOW TO READ IN SCIENCE

This is a science selection, and you should read it differently from the way you read the story about Cal Rodgers or the social studies selection. This selection explains processes which make an airplane fly.

The instructions tell you how to read this selection and any other science material that describes a process.

1. Study the diagram. Read the names of the parts. Then try to name them without rereading the labels.
2. Read all the headings in the selection to find out what three processes will be described.
3. Read the section under the first heading. Read just one sentence at a time and think about it. Look back at the diagram often to find the part or parts of an airplane mentioned. Try to understand just how these parts work, as described in the sentences. After reading the entire section in this way, try to explain to yourself without looking at the book just how the process takes place.
4. Read each of the other sections in the same way that you read the first one.
5. Do Activities 1 and 2.

You have just read an article about the development of airplanes. Do you know how an airplane engine works? Why does an airplane stay up? What makes an airplane move forward? You can learn something about the subject by reading the selection below.

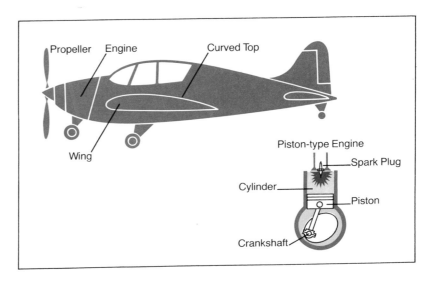

How An Airplane Works _____

Written for this book
by Leo Schneider.

People who invent or improve airplanes must have a great deal of scientific information. They must know many facts about the air, and they must understand how machinery works. Some of this information is explained to you in this selection.

What Makes an Airplane Stay Up?

There is air all around our earth, up to a height of about 500 miles (800 kilometers). This air presses on all objects. It

---

propeller (prə pel′ēr), a device consisting of a revolving hub with blades for propelling a boat, ship, or airplane.

cylinder (sil′ən dēr), a hollow or solid body shaped like a roller.

crankshaft (kraŋk′shaft′), a long, slender part turned by a crank.

presses equally hard downward, upward, and sideways. Suppose that you could find some way of lessening the downward pressure of the air on this book and at the same time that you could increase the upward pressure. The book would be lifted upward, right out of your hands! The wings of airplanes are shaped to make this lift happen.

The top of each wing is arched, while the bottom is flat. As the plane rolls along the ground, the air rushes over the wing. You can see that the air rushing over the top has a longer way to go to reach the back of the wing because it must travel over the arch. You might expect that this air would take longer in getting to the back, but it doesn't. It gets there at exactly the same time as the air at the bottom. That means it must have moved faster, for it had a longer way to go. This faster movement lessens the air pressure on top of the wing. As the plane races faster and faster along the ground, the air pressure on top of the wing decreases so much that the plane is pushed upward. This upward push is called "lift."

Most of the lift of an airplane wing comes from the arched top of the wing. However, the wing is set at a slight upward slant, so that the air hitting the bottom causes some lift there, too. As long as the plane keeps moving forward fast enough, the lifting force will keep it up in the air.

What Makes an Airplane Move?

In most small airplanes, one propeller with two or more blades pulls the plane along. Some large airplanes have four or more propellers.

If you look at the diagram carefully, you will see that the propeller blades are twisted. To move a plane, you must first start the motor. Then the propeller blades spin, and the twist pushes the air *backward*. This forces the airplane *forward*.

The forward force pulls the plane along at high speed.

How Is the Power Provided?

Power from a gasoline engine causes the propeller to spin. The engine is made up of a number of *cylinders*. Each cylinder looks like a soup can with one end removed. Inside the cylinder is another "can," called a *piston*. The piston is just slightly narrower than the cylinder, so the piston can slide back and forth inside the cylinder. The bottom end of the piston is connected to a *crankshaft*, which is forced to rotate by the sliding of the piston. The propeller is at the end of the crankshaft, so it also spins around.

The pistons operate according to a *four-stroke cycle*. The first stroke, the *intake* stroke, is a downward movement of the piston that draws a gas-air mixture into the cylinder. The second stroke, the *compression* stroke, is an upward movement of the piston that squeezes the mixture into the top of the cylinder. At the end of this stroke, the spark plug shoots a spark into the gas-air mixture. The *expansion*, or power, stroke follows. The spark causes the compressed gas-air mixture to explode and push the piston downward with great force. The piston then turns the shaft, which turns the propeller, which moves the plane. The *exhaust* stroke is an upward movement to push the burned gases out of the cylinder.

ACTIVITY 1

Drawing an Airplane Wing

1. On your own paper, draw an airplane wing with the arched top and the slight upward slant of the flat bottom.

2. Draw a dotted line showing the path traveled by air rushing over the top of the wing.

3. Draw another dotted line showing the path traveled by air rushing under the wing.

4. Explain why air pressure is less on top of the wing.

ACTIVITY 2

Explaining a Process

On your paper explain what happens to make the airplane move from the time the plane is standing still until it is moving very fast. (You should have four steps in your process.)

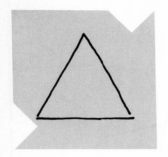

HOW TO READ IN MATHEMATICS

Reading mathematics calls for skills that are different from those needed in reading literature, social studies, or science. For one thing, every word is important. Skipping a word that you don't know will not work in mathematics. If you come to a word that you don't recognize, be sure to look it up.

Another special feature of mathematics is that the text mixes words with numerals and other kinds of symbols. The "other kinds of symbols" may be letters such as n, x, d, and so on. They may be signs such as $>$, $<$, π. They may be abbreviations such as cm. or qt. Numerals, letters, and signs may be found not only in sentences but also by themselves in equations or in formulas. You must know how to read all of these.

Then there are geometric figures. You must be able to recognize the triangle and the pyramid, the cube and the cylinder, and many other figures. All of this is part of reading in mathematics.

You must read explanations carefully. Then there are directions to be read and carried out exactly. In the lesson that follows, you will practice reading and working with formulas.

Look at the pictures of aircraft in the selections in this Unit. In articles about airplanes, helicopters, balloons, and rockets, numbers are frequently used. The mathematics sections of this book will help you read this kind of material.

Mathematical Formulas in Science

Written for this book
by William L. Schaaf.

Scientists today use mathematics more than ever before. They could not design a jet plane or a spaceship without using mathematical *formulas.*

Some of these formulas may seem strange. For example, to figure out the amount of drag on an airplane wing, they use the formula

$$D = kSV^2.$$

Here the letter S stands for the surface area of the wing, the V stands for the air speed or velocity, and k is some particular number, depending upon the wing design. The ^{2} above and to the right of V shows that V is to be multiplied by itself.

Some formulas are more complicated. For example,

$$S = 2\pi r^2 + 2\pi rh$$

represents the total surface area of a closed circular cylinder, such as a tomato can.

Other formulas, although they look quite simple, represent very important ideas, such as Einstein's famous formula, $E = mc^2$, which first suggested the large

formula (fôr'mū lə), a rule or principle expressed in mathematical symbols.

drag (drag), anything that holds something back, as air holds back a moving airplane.

complicated (kom'plə kāt'id), made up of many parts, hard to solve.

Einstein (īn'stīn), American physicist who developed the theory of relativity.

amount of energy in an atom.

Let us look at some simple formulas.

1. Consider a square whose sides are each 3 inches long. Since there are four sides, the perimeter of the square (or "distance around it") is 4 times the length of one side, or $4 \times 3 \, (= 12 \text{ inches})$. On your paper, write the perimeter of a square whose side is
    a. 10 centimeters **b.** 15 feet

2. Do you see that if the side of a square is s units long, then the perimeter (P) is $4 \times s$? We write: $P = 4 \times s$, or $P = 4s$. We read it: "P equals four times s."

3. If the price of one book is $2, then the cost of 3 books is $3 \times \$2 \, (= \$6)$. If the price of one book is $5, then the cost of 4 books is $4 \times \$5 \, (= \$20)$. Do you see that if the price of one article is p dollars, then the cost (C) of n articles is $n \times p$ dollars? We write: $C = n \times p$ or $C = np$. We read it: "Cost equals n times p."

4. Sometimes we must divide when using a formula. If both sides of the equation are divided by the same number, the equation remains equal. For example: If $A = lw$, find w when $A = 54$ and $l = 9$. Since $A = lw$, then $54 = 9w$ or $9w = 54$.
    $$\frac{\cancel{9}w}{\cancel{9}} = \frac{54}{9} \text{ or } w = 6$$

ACTIVITY 1   Using Formulas

1. a. If $P = 4s$, find P when $s = 12$ centimeters.
   b. Find P when $s = 20$ meters.

2. a. If $C = np$, find C when $p = \$3.00$ and $n = 12$.
   b. Now find C when $p = \$1.50$ and $n = 10$.

3. a. If $D = RT$, find D (distance) when R (rate) $= 45$ miles per hour and T (time) $= 3$ hours.
   b. Find D when $R = 88$ feet a second and $T = 2\frac{1}{2}$ seconds.

4. a. If $A = lw$, find A (area) when w (width) $= 3$ inches and l (length) $= 5$ inches.
   b. Find A when $l = 12$ feet and $w = 9$ feet.

5. a. If $F = ma$, find F when $m = 250$ and $a = 4$.
   b. Find F when $m = 2,000$ and $a = 8$.

ACTIVITY 2   More Practice with Formulas

1. In the formula $A = lw$, find l when $A = 96$ and $w = 8$.

2. In the formula $C = np$, find p when the cost C is $\$72$ and the number of articles n is 8.

3. In the formula $C = np$, find n when $C = \$112$ and $p = \$8$.

4. In the formula $D = RT$, find the time (T) required to travel a distance (D) of 180 miles at the rate (R) of 60 miles an hour.

5. In the formula $D = RT$, find R when $T = 3$ hours and $D = 75$ miles.

Finding Main Ideas

In each of the following paragraphs there is one main idea. As you read each paragraph you will find one sentence that is more important than the rest. This sentence will give you the main idea of the entire paragraph.

Very often this main idea is given in the first sentence of the paragraph. At other times the main idea may come in the middle of a paragraph or at the very end of a paragraph. In other words, the main idea may come anywhere in a paragraph. You should be able to find the main idea in a paragraph wherever it may come. See how well you can do this in reading these paragraphs.

1. Read each paragraph carefully.
2. Decide which sentence gives the main idea of the paragraph.
3. Write the main idea sentence on your paper.

In the first paragraph, the main idea has been underlined for you.

1. When cooling temperatures signal the coming of fall weather, the land snail prepares to hibernate. It searches for a nice winter resting place under fallen leaves, or it may burrow under the surface of the soil. Here it sends out a cement-like substance that closes the shell opening. This protects it from the cold. And so, comfortably in its shell, the snail goes to sleep and awaits the spring. In summer the snail sometimes seals itself from the heat. So you see that the snail does its own air conditioning.

2. Banana plants grow very rapidly. In about a year's time they reach their full height of 10 to 25 feet (3 to 7.5 meters). Within ten months after a banana plant has sprouted, flower buds appear on the top of its stalk. As the buds grow larger, the stalk bends over and hangs downward. Soon a heavy purple petal rolls back on each bud. Inside the bud can be seen a row of tiny flowers. These flowers become little green bananas. The bananas grow in bunches. Within three or four months the bananas are ready for shipping. They are cut down from the plants and are then sent to countries where bananas do not grow.

3. Do you know where the word *cereal* came from? The ancient Romans prayed to a goddess named Ceres. Ceres was the Roman goddess of agriculture. The Romans believed that Ceres guarded their food plants and thus helped the farmers. She was also responsible for the growing season. When she was happy the crops grew well. When she was unhappy the crops didn't grow. Once a year a festival was held in her honor, and it was called the *Cerealia*. From the name *Ceres* and the name of her festival came the word *cereal*. We use the word to describe various kinds of grain from grass-like plants, such as oats, corn, wheat, and rice.

4. A firefly winks its light in the summer night. A bird migrates thousands of miles to its winter home in the south. A dolphin swims fast enough to outrace some speedboats. Each of these animals knows how to do something people can do. A firefly appears to burn something to create light. People do the same thing with fire or with electric light bulbs. A bird can travel great distances. So can people with their airplanes or ships. And a dolphin speeds through water. People can also speed through water by means of a motorboat. In each instance, however, there is a big difference between animals and people. Animals can create light, travel in air, and speed through water by themselves, but people must have many aids in order to do these things.

Critical and Creative Reading: Fact and Opinion

How do you know when to question or doubt something and when to believe it?

In general, you can believe a fact, but you should question an opinion. A *fact* is something that can be proved to be true; an *opinion* is something that someone thinks is true.

Usually you should question an opinion until you have proof that the opinion is right. Often you can tell when a person is giving an opinion. If you find such words as *think, thought, believe, says, said, told,* and so on, you can be fairly sure that an opinion is being expressed.

When looking for facts or to see if something really happened, look for names and dates. Look for the proof of the statement.

When you judge or evaluate what you read, you are doing *critical* reading. When you are adding new ideas of your own, you are doing *creative* reading. You will have a chance to do both of these kinds of reading while working with the following articles.

Listening in on Other Worlds

"The United States can eavesdrop on more than one intelligent civilization elsewhere in the universe any time we are ready to set up the gear." This is what Bernard M. Oliver, a famous electronics engineer, told a crowd of people. He proposed building one thousand to ten thousand radio-telescopes. "By coupling these telescopes together," he said, we could "virtually listen to creation itself."

Write the answers to these questions.
1. Which three words in the paragraph above indicate that Mr. Oliver's theory was *opinion?*
2. Did Bernard Oliver prove that by putting thousands of telescopes together we could listen in on other worlds?
3. Did he say that anyone else had done this successfully?
4. Is this a statement of fact or opinion?

Goddard and Rockets

Robert H. Goddard was born in October of 1882. When only seventeen, he became interested in rockets. After receiving his Bachelor of Science degree in 1908, he became a college instructor and continued his studies. He was convinced that there was a way for rockets to travel to the moon and to other planets. By 1909 he had the idea of using a powerful liquid fuel in a new kind of rocket, called a step rocket (one rocket carried by another). He began his experiments in 1914.

Dr. Goddard wrote an article called "A Method of Reaching Extreme Altitudes" that was published in 1919. Most people thought his theories were silly, but he received money to continue his research. In 1926 he launched the first successful liquid-fuel rocket. Dr. Goddard took out many patents on his rockets. Today it is almost impossible to design, construct, or launch a rocket without making use of a Goddard patent. He should be called the "Father of Modern Rocketry."

1. Did Goddard have an unproved theory only?
2. What did he do that proved his theory?
3. What three things did Goddard do that earned for him the title "Father of Modern Rocketry"?

Angel Hair

A material called "Angel Hair" has fallen from the skies in many places. This material is white and looks something like cobwebs. It drapes itself like a blanket over housetops, trees, bushes, and telephone wires. It sometimes falls in strips ten yards or more in length. It disappears completely in a rather short time. It is said that "Angel Hair" often falls shortly after flying saucers are seen. For this reason many people believe that the substance falls from flying saucers.

Some people think that it is material blown from cloth factories. These people reason that this material is made of left-over woolen or nylon fibers that such factories have thrown away. Others think it is made up of chemicals used for seeding clouds to make it rain.

1. Has anyone *proved* what "Angel Hair" is?
2. Have you any idea about what "Angel Hair" may be? If so, what is your idea?
3. Is the underlined sentence a fact or an opinion?

The Blackout of 1965

On November 9, 1965, a complete blackout of lights covered the northeastern corner of the United States. Millions of people were without lights from late afternoon until the next morning. It was as if a great black blanket had been thrown over all cities, towns, and homes.

People did not agree about the cause of this blackout. However, two people were driving from Syracuse to Humbert. On the way they saw what they thought was a flying saucer. Shortly afterwards they heard their car radio saying that a blackout had covered the whole area. It is reported that others think they saw flying saucers that same evening.

1. Are you given proof that flying saucers caused the blackout?
2. What do you think might have caused it?
3. a. Is the first sentence fact or opinion?
   b. Is it fact or opinion that other flying saucers were sighted?

Writing Titles for Paragraphs

When studying, it is often helpful to sum up the topics of paragraphs by writing a title for each paragraph. In this lesson, you will have practice in writing titles for paragraphs. Use your own words to sum up the topic of the paragraph.

1. Read each paragraph carefully.
2. Think of the paragraph as if it were an entire story or an entire article.
3. Write a title on your paper for each paragraph. A title for the first one is written for you.

1. *Wild Life at Cape Canaveral*

Cape Canaveral is always bustling with the excitement of missiles, rockets, and tracking stations. Even so, wildlife is still to be found there. Workers at the Cape often see wild rabbits and armadillos. Hawks, sea gulls, vultures, and pelicans are seen in great numbers. Even a few alligators still manage to live in their old homes. One year, members of an Atlas launch crew discovered a ten-foot alligator sunning itself in the entrance to their blockhouse. None of them dared to go in past the alligator, so they called the fire department. The fire fighters lassoed the alligator, carried it off, and put it into the nearby Banana River.

2. Wimpey was a tiny ape born in a zoo. When he was four months old, his mother disowned him. She refused to have anything more to do with him. So one of the zoo keepers took him home and fed him milk and fruit. Wimpey soon got used to his new home. However, he was very lonely. Then one day the family's Great Dane dog, Prince, went by the box in which Wimpey was sleeping. He stopped to lick Wimpey's head and back. Wimpey was very happy. He had found a friend. He wasn't alone any longer. From that time on, Wimpey usually slept snuggled up next to Prince.

3. In Houston, Texas, there is an old box elder tree that appears to cry. It "weeps" steadily. If you stand under this tree in the spring or summer when it has leaves, you can feel the water falling like rain. When the leaves fall off in autumn, the tree rains harder than ever. Many people have attempted to explain this. One scientist says that when the tree cries, it is really giving off the water that it has absorbed with its roots.

4. Oceans contain great wealth that we don't yet know how to recover. Every cubic mile of sea water contains millions of tons of dissolved salt and minerals. How can these be separated from the water and used? Mysterious-looking masses containing magnesium, cobalt, nickel, and copper cover miles of ocean floor. With fresh water becoming scarcer, there is a need for taking salt and other minerals out of the sea water. Chemists and engineers are working on all these problems.

Writing a Title for an Article

First, read the article below and write a subhead for each part. Think of the subhead as a title for that part. After you have read the article and written the subheads, then write a title for the entire article.

(Title)

There have been several outstanding singers in America during the twentieth century. One of these is Marian Anderson.

(Subhead 1)

Marian Anderson was born in Philadelphia, Pennsylvania, on February 17, 1902. Her parents were black, and they were very poor.

She joined the Union Baptist Church when she was six years old. Her first musical training was singing in the choir of this church.

Later, she took lessons from a well-known voice teacher. He entered her in a contest of the New York Philharmonic Orchestra. She won first place among the 300 contestants.

(Subhead 2)

There were several years, however, during which Marian had a great struggle. Poverty was one of her problems. Voice lessons and training are expensive. To go on singing tours also costs a great deal of money. Travel is costly. Besides paying for herself, she had to pay for someone to accompany her on the piano. Then, too, a singer has to have beautiful gowns to wear on the stage. All of this made it very difficult for a poor girl like Marian Anderson to go ahead with her career.

At this time there was also discrimination against Miss Anderson because she was black. This, of course, was entirely unfair and unjust. It made her very sad. But she was determined to succeed. Regardless of the problems, she kept on trying.

(Subhead 3)

Real success came in 1933 when Miss Anderson went to Europe. Upon her return she was asked to sing at the White House and the Metropolitan Opera House. Her well-earned success had come at last.

But success did not change her great warmth and kindness to everyone. She did many wonderful things for her country. The high point in her life came when she was appointed as a U.S. delegate to the United Nations.

Philharmonic Orchestra (fil här mon′ik ôr′kis trə), the name of a musical organization.

Metropolitan (met′rə pol′ə t′n), name of a famous opera company located in New York City.

How to Read Fast

You will have a great deal of reading to do in your grade this year. You can do more of it in less time if you learn to read rapidly.

Perhaps you have been told about some habits which keep a person from reading fast. Do you have any of these habits? Check yourself by answering "Yes" or "No" to these questions:

1. Do you move your lips when reading silently?
2. Do you point to words with your finger as you read?
3. Do you move your head from side to side as you read?
4. Do you often go back over a line of print because you think you've missed something?
5. Do you read one word at a time?

If you answered "Yes" to any of these questions, start at once to break the habit.

If you move your lips, hold your finger over them, or hold a piece of paper between your lips while you are reading. Then if your lips move you will know it and can stop them.

If you point to words, hold the two sides of your book, one side with your left hand, the other side with the right hand. Then you won't have a free finger to use in pointing while reading.

If you move your head, place your chin in one hand, and hold your head still.

If you glance back often, it may be because you can't pronounce some of the words or because you don't get the meaning of certain words or phrases or sentences. The work you do in this book in word pronunciation and meanings should help you with this problem.

If you read no more than one or two or three words at a time, you must learn to take in more words at each glance as your eyes travel across the lines of print.

If you read fairly fast now, you can learn to read still faster. The secret of fast reading is to take in whole groups of words at a glance. Read in thought units and force your eyes along the lines of print as fast as you can make them go. Anyone who practices doing these two things can increase reading speed.

If you are using this book alone, without a teacher to help you with timing, use a watch with a second hand for timing yourself. If you haven't such a watch, perhaps you will find that the school clock has a second hand and you can use that. If you do not have either a watch or a clock with a second hand, do the best you can with a minute hand.

Start on an *even* minute, such as 5 minutes after 10:00 or 20 minutes after 2:00. On a piece of paper, write your "Beginning Time" when you are ready to start the story and your "Ending Time" when you have finished.

The Wonderful Discovery on Mars

Written for this book
by Enid Johnson.

It was the year 2001 A.D. For thirty years, explorers from Earth had journeyed into space, but no one had as yet managed to land on Mars. Colonel Dixon, a space explorer, had already traveled to the moon. He was planning to fly to Mars now, and he was taking Mrs. Dixon and their son Tom, in addition to his crew.

Colonel Dixon was hoping to solve the problems of living on Mars so that he and his family might be able to remain for a while on the planet. He was even more concerned about later explorers. If he could find a solution to some of the problems of living on Mars, other explorers would be able to stay there long enough to collect needed information about this planet.

The two problems Colonel Dixon hoped to solve concerned climate and food. He knew the climate was so cold that human beings from Earth could not live there for long without freezing. He also had been told by scientists that it was doubtful that any crops could be grown on Mars.

Colonel Dixon believed that the white patches at the poles were made of tiny flakes of very hard snow. He also believed that the lines seen by astronomers were canals, and that the icecaps melted in the summer and filled these canals with water. He believed that the green and red-brown areas on Mars were plants. So with these ideas in mind, the Dixon family zoomed off to explore Mars.

Soon after their spaceship had left Earth, Tom discovered that Jackie, his pet dog, had stowed away on board. His father was annoyed, but it was too late to do anything about it.

It was an exciting moment for the Dixon family when they landed on Mars. They found the canals that Colonel Dixon expected to find. He thought they proved that humanlike creatures with intelligence had lived on the planet. But the canals were dry. There were no lakes or rivers— only rocky, waterless plains stretched out before them.

The crew dug deep into the surface of Mars, built some crude underground huts for shelter and unpacked their supplies. Soon Mrs. Dixon had everyone feeling comfortable and very much at home. "Now if we could only find some water," said Colonel Dixon.

He was convinced that the famous canals had water in them for three months in the summer when the icecaps at the poles on Mars melted. But what had be-come of the creatures who had built the canals? Colonel Dixon explored many acres of the planet and found nothing else to prove that Martians had ever lived there. "Perhaps they built spaceships and moved to another planet hundreds of years ago," he said.

Every day, Tom took Jackie and went to watch the crew exploring the surface of Mars. Tom was getting used to being so light that he seemed to be almost floating over the ground. On Mars, he weighed one third of his normal weight on Earth.

One day, when the members of the crew were exploring nearby, Tom suddenly realized Jackie was missing. He started hunting frantically for his pet. After a while he found Jackie digging away in some loose light soil behind an enormous rock. The crew had not dug here, so Tom called his father to bring the crew with their atomic drills. After hours of digging, they came to several very large underground storage tanks. What appeared to be pipelines led away from the tanks.

By following the pipelines, they came to a vast meadow, where peculiar looking plants were growing. The plants looked something like the mosses we find growing here on Earth. Colonal Dixon picked one of these plants and decided to take a sample taste. "Surprisingly good!" he said.

"Those early Martians must have been wonderful engineers. See, they managed to pipe water first from their canals to the tanks, and then to this meadow. Probably some thousands of years ago the planet was shaken by what we would call an earthquake, and the tanks were covered up.

"Thanks to Jackie," continued Colonel Dixon, "we have discovered the method they used to provide themselves with water during the months when their canals were dry, and how they provided themselves with food to eat. We have lived comfortably in our underground homes for quite a few days. Our journey has been successful. Back to Earth tomorrow!"

27

Checking Your Understanding

While it is important for you to increase your speed of reading, you should never read so fast that you fail to get the meaning. On your paper, write the answers to these questions to see how well you understand the story.

1. What two problems did Colonel Dixon hope to solve?
2. What was his theory concerning the white patches on Mars?
3. What was his belief about the lines which astronomers have seen on Mars?
4. What was his theory in regard to the green and red-brown areas on Mars?
5. What kind of land did they find when they landed on Mars?

6. Where did they build huts?
7. What did they find underground?
8. What was Colonel Dixon's idea about how the pipes and tanks had become covered with earth?
9. What was his idea about what had happened to the Martians?
10. What three discoveries made him satisfied with his trip?

Give yourself a score of 10 for each correct answer. The total is your comprehension score. It tells how well you understood the story.

The following explanation will help you find your speed (the number of words per minute you read). After you find your speed, record your comprehension score on the last line of the chart.

Checking Your Speed

Finding your "Total Reading Time"

On your paper subtract your beginning time from your ending time. Suppose you started at 10 minutes after ten o'clock and you finished at 13 minutes and 30 seconds after ten. Then you would find your reading time in this way:

	Hr.	Min.	Sec.
Ending time:	10	13	30
Beginning time:	10	10	
Total Reading Time:			3 min. 30 sec.

Now change the total reading time into seconds:

$$60 \times 3 = 180 \qquad 180 + 30 = 210$$

Finding the Number of Words per Minute

There are 744 words in this story. You would use the formula below to find the number of words per minute you read in this story.

$$\frac{\text{No. words}}{\text{No. seconds}} \, \frac{744}{210} \times 60 = \frac{212 \text{ words}}{\text{per minute}}$$

Use this same plan in finding the number of words per minute *you* read while working with this article. Copy this chart on your paper and work out your score.

	Hr.	Min.	Sec.
Ending time:	____	____	____
Beginning time:	____	____	____
Total Time:	____	____	____

No. words: No. seconds: $\left(\dfrac{744}{}\right) \times 60 =$ _____ **WPM**

Comprehension Score: _____

Reviewing Vowels

Do you still have trouble in working out the pronunciation of new words?

There will be some new and difficult words in the books that you will use this year. You will need to look up some of these words in a dictionary, but it takes time to look up *all* of them. You should be so skillful in working out word pronunciations that you can do this by yourself when you first meet the words on the pages of your books.

It is a good thing to take stock at this time of the year to find out just how much you do know about pronouncing words, and what you don't know.

One of the most important things for you to know is the sounds of different letters and groups of letters. You have had work with sounds of letters in the past. Perhaps you have forgotten about this work or have become careless in using it. So sounds will be reviewed in this book.

You know, of course, that the vowels are *a, e, i, o, u,* and sometimes *y;* but *y* as a vowel has the sound of long *e,* or long *i,* or short *i.*

A. Finding Words That Begin with a Vowel. In each of the boxes below there is one word that begins with a vowel. Find that word in each box and write it on your paper.

1. ankle rocket silver	**2.** plane invent beetle	**3.** effect ranch scream	**4.** fact river odd
5. engine transport reason	**6.** flight travel era	**7.** product design unit	**8.** glider industry balloon

B. Finding Words That End with a Vowel. In each of the boxes below there is one word that ends with a vowel. Find that word in each box and write it on your paper.

1. subject process extra	**2.** jolly diagram section	**3.** movement propeller coffee	**4.** crank piston saliva
5. plasma demand bomber	**6.** recent modern stereo	**7.** problem special radio	**8.** travel volcano material

Reviewing the Long and Short Vowel Sounds _____

You will remember that the most common vowel sounds are the *long sounds* and the *short sounds*. Key words are given for these sounds in the list shown below. When you look up words in most dictionaries you sometimes find a bar above a vowel, like this: ā. This means that the vowel is long. A vowel in the dictionary has the short sound if it has no mark above it, like this: a.

Long Vowel Sounds	Short Vowel Sounds
1. ā as in *late*	**8.** a as in *act*
2. ē as in *see*	**9.** e as in *end*
3. ī as in *ice*	**10.** i as in *hit*
4. ō as in *no*	**11.** o as in *dot*
5. ū as in *use*	**12.** u as in *up*
6. y as in *cry* (krī)	**13.** y as in *gym* (jim)
7. y as in *only* (ōn lē)	

Number your paper from 1 to 30. Referring to the table, describe the long or short vowel sound in each word. Remember to respell *y* as *i* or *e*. The first two have been done for you.

Long or Short *a*

1. age *a* as in *late*
2. land *a* as in *act*
3. strap
4. save
5. lake

Long or Short *e*

6. best
7. we
8. fed
9. cedar
10. rest

Long or Short *i*

11. tin
12. lick
13. size
14. fish
15. time

Long or Short *o*

16. mold
17. flock
18. snow
19. job
20. gold

Long or Short *u*

21. mule
22. pup
23. rush
24. union
25. value

y as Long *e*, or Long or Short *i*

26. fly
27. ready
28. system
29. why
30. tiny

Applying Vowel Principles _____

You already know the vowel principles listed below:

A. When a one-syllable word contains two vowels one of which is final *e*, the first vowel is usually long and the final *e* is silent, as in *space*.

B. When there is only one vowel in a word and that vowel does not come at the end of the word, the vowel is usually short, as in *flat* or as in *mud*.

C. When two vowels come together in a one-syllable word, the first vowel is usually long and the second vowel is usually silent, as in *hail*.

_____

See if you can apply these vowel principles in the work below.

A. Number your paper from 1 to 10. Write the letter of the vowel principle that applies to each word.

1. Jane	**6.** beast
2. groan	**7.** luck
3. phrase	**8.** goal
4. team	**9.** fact
5. task	**10.** main

B. Several pairs of vowels represent the same long sound. For example:

> *ay, ai,* and *ey* all sound like long *a* in *hay, tail, they.*
> *ea, ei,* and *ee* all sound like long *e* in *each, receive, sheep.*
> *ie, uy* both sound like long *i* in *die, buy.*
> *oa, oe, ou* all sound like long *o* in *coat, Joe, soul, though.*

On your paper, make 4 columns with these headings:

> Long *a*   Long *e*   Long *i*   Long *o*

Write each of these words under the heading that represents the sound of the two vowels that come together within the word.

treat	strain	failure	trail
coal	pie	leap	deal
speed	leave	ceiling	goal
train	tried	tie	hoe
dried	grain	oats	lie
roam	hail	dough	die

31

Reviewing Consonants

Words are made up of both vowels and consonants. You must be able to recognize consonants quickly, as well as vowels.

You have just reviewed the vowels: *a, e, i, o, u* and sometimes *y.* You know, of course, that all of the other letters in the alphabet are consonants. See how quickly you can recognize the consonants when you see them.

A. Write the alphabet and draw one line under each consonant.

B. Look at each of these pictures. The name of each picture begins with a consonant sound. Say its name to yourself. With what sound does the name start? Find the letter beneath the picture that stands for that sound. Write that letter on your paper.

Did you miss the sounds of any of the consonants with which the names of the pictures begin? If so, think of as many words as you can which begin with each sound you missed. Make a list of words for each sound that you missed, and think of the sound of the beginning consonant as you write each word.

C. In the test you just took, you were to write only the consonant with which the word *began*. It is important also that you know the sound of a consonant when it comes at the *end* of a word.

Make two columns on your paper—mark one *Beginning* and the other *Ending*.

Say the names of the pictures in each of the boxes below. Find pictures of two words in each box in which the same letter sound comes at the beginning of one of the words and at the end of the other. Write these words in the correct column and underline the consonant letter that is the same in both.

Working with Science Words

The words and phrases appear often in science textbooks. You will meet them very frequently in your reading both in and out of school. Make sure you know how to pronounce these words and what they mean.

Study the pronunciation of each of these words or phrases. Say each word to yourself, pronouncing it distinctly. Then read the meaning of the word or phrase and think about it.

---

automation (ô′təm mā′shən), control of machines by other machines instead of directly by human operators.

detergent (di tûr′jənt), a cleanser used in place of soap.

electronics (i lek tron′iks), the branch of physics that deals with electrons in motion.

fluorine (floo′ə rēn), a substance placed in drinking water to prevent tooth decay.

hormones (hôr′mōnz), chemicals made by glands in the body.

plastic (plas′tik), a substance manufactured in industry which can be shaped when

hot and which becomes hard when cooled.

satellite (sat′ə līt′), a small planet that revolves around a large planet; a metal sphere launched by a rocket to orbit around the earth.

supersonic (soo′pēr son′ik), having speed greater than that of sound.

synthetic textiles (sin thet′ik teks′tlz), cloth which is manufactured from various raw materials; nylon, for example, is made of materials found in coal, air, and water.

virus (vī′rəs), the smallest living thing which causes diseases.

See how well you understand the meanings of the words you have been studying. On your own paper, write the correct word to complete each sentence below. Add *s* if necessary.

1. Airplanes today are able to travel faster than sound at _____ speeds.

2. In college Tom is studying a branch of physics called _____.

3. Glands produce various _____.

4. Many people have lost their jobs because so many machines are now run by _____.

5. Some scientists believe that the common cold is caused by a type of _____.

6. Many cities are putting _____ in drinking water to prevent tooth decay.

7. Mrs. Perez uses a _____ to do her laundry each week.

8. Many combs, dishes, and toys are made from a substance called _____, which can be shaped when hot and hardens when cool.

9. Rockets have sent up small metal spheres called _____, which orbit the earth.

10. Clothing manufacturers use many of the new materials created by people. These new materials are called _____.

2
Northland Adventure, Alaska

In the last story you read you thought about character. Another element of a story that always involves character is conflict. You know that conflict is the problem faced by the characters in a story. In some stories, you will find that the problem is caused by a situation. In other stories, the conflict may be a problem between two characters. Still a third kind of conflict may be a problem within one of the characters. As the story is developed, you will find the characters trying to solve the problem—trying to resolve the conflict. As this happens, you will learn more about the characters in seeing how they handle the problem.

As you read this story, think about conflict. Before you begin, read the questions in Activity 3, page 39. Think about these questions as you read the story.

Record your beginning and ending time.

Have you ever wanted to prove yourself, so that you would be accepted by some person or group? In the next story, you will read about someone who wanted to do that but couldn't. How he tried to solve his problem makes an interesting story.

Tea

Written for this book by Irene Elmer
from material by William W. Elmer.

I knew Single-Eye Charlie back in 1916; I was up in Alaska then, doing a little placer mining. It was twenty years after the gold rush, and the big companies had taken over most of the old claims, but men were still heading up North, hoping to make their fortunes in the mines. I was a strong young fellow then—in those days I had more brawn than sense—so I went up to make my fortune, too.

I was working a claim on a little creek that fed into the Chistochina River, south of Mt. Kimball, in the Alaska Range. I had found a little gold—enough to live on— nothing much. That's the way it mostly was. But I was always hoping for the big strike; and I was young and didn't mind hard work. It was hard work, too, placer mining was. First you'd dam up your creek and you'd build your sluice box and your flumes. Flumes are channels for carrying the water; and the sluice box—that's a long channel with riffles—little strips of wood set crosswise all along.

Well, next you'd shovel your gravel into the sluice box, and you'd let the water out of the dam. The water runs down the sluice box, carrying the gravel along with it, and the heaviest gravel—the gravel that

---

placer mining (plās′ĕr min′ing), mining of deposits by washing or dredging.

brawn (brôn), strong, well-developed muscles.

sluice box (slo͞os boks), an artificial channel for water.

cheechako (chē chä′kō), an Alaskan word for newcomer, tenderfoot.

has gold in it—sticks in the riffles. That's called the concentrate. You'd pan the concentrate by hand to separate out the gold. That's the way we did it then. It's all done by machine now.

After a hard day's work you might end up with a quarter of an ounce of gold; in those days that would be worth maybe four or five dollars. Of course, some claims didn't bring in anything. But in '96 some claims were bringing in one hundred, two hundred dollars a day. That's why, even twenty years later, men were still heading up North to stake new claims.

. . . But I started to tell you about Single-Eye Charlie.

Single-Eye Charlie was a Matanuska Indian who kept the general store in the nearest village. I'd go there once a month to buy supplies. It wasn't much of a village, but after a month in the bush it looked like New York City to me, and I was in no rush to trudge back 45 miles (72 kilometers) to

camp, where I might not see another soul for days. So I used to hang around the store and talk to Charlie.

He spoke good English, and I think he sort of liked me, but it's hard to tell. I'll tell you the story and you can judge for yourself. He'd been born up there, of course, long before the gold rush, and he wasn't above playing a joke on a *cheechako* like me. Anyone who hadn't been born there was a *cheechako* to Charlie.

It was always the same. I'd sit down beside the stove, and old Charlie wouldn't say anything, but he'd pour me out a cup of tea from the coffeepot he kept there on the stove. He kept that pot going night and day, and strong? I've never tasted anything like that tea. You could have used it to tan reindeer hide.

Charlie, he'd sit and watch me, and I'd try to drink it—but I just couldn't. And all the time Charlie was watching me, we'd be talking about something else.

"You find lots of gold up there, Bill?"

"Not yet. But I'll strike it rich, you'll see. I panned a two-dollar nugget yesterday."

"You do better soon, maybe, when ice leave creek; water not so cold then."

"Cold doesn't bother me, Charlie—why I don't even feel the cold."

Charlie, he wouldn't say anything, but he'd reach for the pot of tea and start to fill my cup, pretending not to notice that I hadn't touched what he'd given me the first time.

"How long sluice box you got now, Bill?"

"Oh, about ten feet (3 meters)."

"Still too short, maybe."

That's the way our conversations went. When I'd finally get up and go out to the lean-to to put on my pack, my tea would still be sitting there by the stove.

Charlie never said a word. He never let on to notice. But a month later, when I came back, he'd do the same thing again.

I was only a kid, and I wanted like anything to prove I was a real Alaskan by drinking Charlie's tea. But I couldn't drink it. It was just plain undrinkable. And Charlie knew it.

After a while, I was just itching to get back at him somehow; and one day I got my chance.

I was cooking supper in my cabin up there above the Chistochina when I heard a shout out on the trail. I looked out; here came an Indian carrying some fish traps. It was Charlie.

He came in. He didn't say anything—just sat down by the stove. I thought, "Charlie, my friend, I'm going to show you a thing or two."

I had a coffeepot full of water on the stove. I got out my tea-tin; it was full. I stood so Charlie couldn't see, and I dumped all the tea into the pot—a pound (.5 kilograms) of tea—my whole month's supply. I put the pot back and stoked up the fire. Pretty soon the tea began to boil. I

listened to it boil for half an hour, while I fried up some hot cakes and bacon.

When supper was ready, I took a look at my tea. I couldn't even see the tea—it was all just soggy tea leaves in there. I tipped the pot, and a big mess of stewed leaves fell into Charlie's cup. The tea itself was black—just black. Drink it? I'd as soon have drunk kerosene. It was the awfulest looking stuff you ever saw.

I handed the cup over to Charlie; he looked at it, but he didn't say anything. I poured a cup for myself, but I didn't drink it, of course. I just sat there and watched Charlie to see what he would do.

He drank it. Yes, sir, he drank that tea. He practically had to chew it to get it down. But his face never changed. I couldn't believe it. I let my supper get cold watching him.

All the time he was drinking his tea, old Charlie never said a word. But when he'd got it all down, still not saying a word, he held out his cup for more.

I couldn't stand it any longer. I said, "This is *my* way of making tea, Charlie. How do you like it?"

Charlie's face never changed. He never even blinked. But I thought I saw a little twinkle in his eye.

"Sometimes I like tea made this way," Charlie said. "Other times, I like it strong."

ACTIVITY 1 — Fact Questions

Write the answers to these questions on your own paper.

1. In what year does this story take place?

2. How long after the Alaska gold rush does it take place?

3. What was Bill doing in Alaska?

4. Why was he doing this?

5. What is a sluice box?

6. What is concentrate?

7. At the time this story takes place, how much was gold worth?

8. What did Single-Eye Charlie do for a living?

9. How often did Bill go into town?

10. How much tea did Bill put into the pot when he made tea for Charlie?

Copy this chart on your paper. Compute and record your WPM as you did on page 28.

Give yourself a score of 10 for each correct answer in Activity 1. This is your comprehension score. Record it on the chart.

	Hr.	**Min.**	**Sec.**
Ending time:	_____	_____	_____
Beginning time:	_____	_____	_____
Total Time:	_____	_____	_____
No. words:			
No. seconds:	$\left(\dfrac{1172}{\quad}\right) \times 60 =$ _____ **WPM**		

Comprehension score: _____

ACTIVITY 2 — Thought Questions

Answer these questions on your paper.

1. When Bill says he had more brawn than sense, what do you think he means? Do you agree?

2. From what you know about placer mining, do you think it would be a profitable way to earn a living? Do you think you would enjoy it? Explain.

3. How do you think Bill felt towards Charlie?

4. How do you think Charlie felt towards Bill?

5. If you had been Charlie, would you have drunk the tea? What else might Charlie have done? What would have happened then?

6. What do you think Bill learned from this episode?

ACTIVITY 3 — Thinking About Conflict

Use your own paper to answer these questions.

1. Is the conflict between a character and a situation, between two characters, within a character, or a combination?

2. What is the conflict?

3. Is the conflict resolved by the end of the story?

**HOW TO READ IN
SOCIAL STUDIES**

In much of the material you will read in social studies, you will find it helpful to think about what you read in terms of cause and effect. A cause is what makes something happen; an effect is what happens as a result of the cause.

Study these examples and think about the cause and the effect in each.

1. Its defeat of the Spanish Armada / marked England's beginnings as a world power.
2. Many Puritans came to America / when there were religious persecutions in England.

In #1, the first part of the sentence gives the cause and the second part gives the effect. In #2, the opposite is true.

As you read the next selection, look especially for causes and effects. Record your beginning and ending time.

Gold isn't the only natural resource that has made people flock to Alaska. Oil is also a great attraction, but transporting it from Alaska is causing great problems. Read the following article to learn more about these problems.

Alaska Pipeline

Written for this book
by Sheila Burns.

A biologist stood on the shore of Cook Inlet in Alaska and watched dead ducks wash up on the beach. Their feathers were covered with oil. Unable to fly, the ducks had struggled and died.

At the same time, a fishing crew pulled some crabs from the icy water. They too were covered with oil. The crew saw a tanker with an oil slick spreading behind it. The tanker was polluting the water for miles around.

In recent years, many new settlers have arrived in Alaska. They hope to become rich from the oil that has been discovered there. But these people have already begun to damage the wilderness and harm the wildlife.

Because Alaska is so enormous and the climate so bitter, it seems impossible for humans to destroy the land. If a map of Alaska were placed over a map of the continental United States, the bottom of the state would be in Florida, and the top somewhere in Minnesota. On Alaska's plains, temperatures drop to 75°F below zero (−59°C) and in summer rise to 100°F above zero (38°C). The land seems too harsh for humans to be able to spoil it.

But, in fact, Alaska is far more fragile than it appears. The tundra, as the land is called, is a thin layer of earth over permanently frozen subsoil. This layer of earth is covered with mosses, grasses, and one-inch high trees. In the short Arctic summer, these small plants bloom, and the surface soil thaws briefly.

During this time, if a truck drives over the soft tundra, it crushes the plants growing there. Because the weather is so harsh, it takes years before they can grow back. For instance, the plants that reindeer eat take twenty-five years to mature.

When their food is destroyed, the reindeer must search for plants in other places. If they cannot find food, they die. The wolves, who feed on the reindeer, die also. In the same way, other animals, birds, and fish will not survive if their food is destroyed.

The newcomers to Alaska have disturbed the wildlife on the ground, in the water, and in the air. Now that oil has become so important, these people may do even more damage in the future. They are building a pipeline, and the oil in it must be kept at about 160°F (71°C). How will that pipeline, pumping hot oil for a distance of 800 miles (1,280 kilometers), affect the tundra? Nobody knows. What happens if the pipe breaks and pours oil for miles around? Nobody knows that either. But the pipeline is being built.

---

fragile (fraj′əl), easily broken, damaged, or destroyed.

The people searching for oil in Alaska have affected not only the wildlife but also the Eskimos and Indians who live there. The Eskimos and Indians have always had a special understanding of the land. From their point of view, there was no ownership of property. There were no boundaries. They believed that the land was a treasure shared by everyone.

Because the Eskimos and Indians did not believe in ownership of land, they did nothing to protect Alaska from the newcomers. Then the natives realized that they had to own the land to keep it from being destroyed. With this new belief, their way of life also began to change. The Eskimos and Indians began to live like the settlers themselves.

Maybe Eskimo and Indian life would have changed even if settlers had not come to Alaska. Maybe animal life would have changed also. No one can be sure.

But the fight for oil in Alaska illustrates a problem that exists throughout the world. The question seems more clear-cut than ever before: How can we create a good life for everyone without damaging the natural world around us?

ACTIVITY 1

Answer these questions on your paper by writing the letter of the effect that follows each cause.

Cause

1. Their feathers were covered with oil, so
2. Because oil has become so important,
3. Because the land in Alaska is so harsh,
4. When reindeer die,
5. Eskimos and Indians did not believe in ownership of land, so

Effect

a. wolves starve and die also.
b. it seems impossible that it could be spoiled.
c. the ducks were unable to fly.
d. they did nothing to protect Alaska from newcomers.
e. people may do more damage to Alaska in the future.

Copy this chart on your paper. Compute and record your WPM as you did on page 28.

Give yourself a score of 20 for each correct answer in Activity 1. This is your comprehension score. Record it on the chart.

	Hr.	Min.	Sec.
Ending time:	_____	_____	_____
Beginning time:	_____	_____	_____
Total time:	_____	_____	_____
No. words: $\left(\dfrac{623}{\text{No. seconds:}}\right) \times 60$ _____ **WPM**			
Comprehension Score: _____			

Use the map of Alaska to answer these questions. Write the answers on your own paper.

1. At what body of water does the pipeline start?

2. After the pipeline crosses the North Slope, through what mountain range does it pass?

3. What river must the pipeline cross?

4. The pipeline passes very close to what large city?

5. Name the city at the southern end of the pipeline.

6. Name three large bodies of water bordering Alaska.

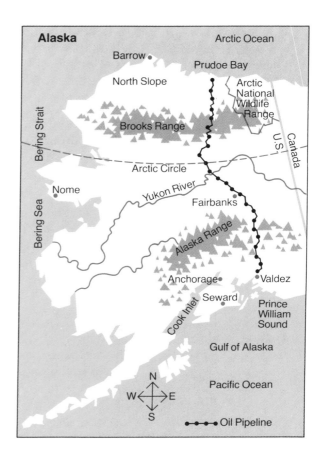

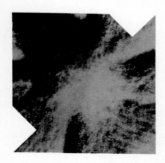

HOW TO READ IN SCIENCE

One of the methods scientists use is the problem-solving method. First they recognize a problem. Then they experiment until they solve the problem. The selection below tells how scientists met some problems in regard to penicillin.

1. First, read the headings. After reading all of them, see if you can state each of the problems.
2. Read the three parts of the selection carefully to (a) review the statement of each problem; (b) find out what was done about it; and (c) find out what the results were.

Usually one cannot read science material as fast as one can read a story or social studies material. Sometimes, however, science material really tells a story of how scientists have met certain problems. Such accounts often are easy to read and can be read rapidly. See how fast you can read this article and still do the three things mentioned above in covering each section.

Scientists are hard at work trying to solve the problems that the Alaska pipeline have created in the environment. In the next article, you will read how scientists solved another problem.

Penicillin

Written for this book
by Irving Zeichner.

Scientists have known for many years that some diseases are caused by germs, or bacteria. Many scientists have tried to find substances that would kill harmful bacteria. Some of these attempts have been successful.

Among the germ killers they discovered are the so-called "wonder drugs."

substance (sub′stans), the matter of which a thing is made.

culture (kul′chĕr), a medium in which bacteria are grown.

meningitis (men′in jī tis), a disease affecting the brain and spinal cord.

Scientists call these drugs *antibiotics*. An antibiotic is a chemical substance made by a living thing that can stop the growth of, or even destroy, bacteria. The best known of these antibiotics is *penicillin*. It was discovered by Dr. Alexander Fleming.

How Could Harmful Bacteria be Controlled? Dr. Fleming, like many other scientists, had been experimenting for some time to learn more about bacteria, and especially about how to control them. He had placed several bacteria cultures in dishes in his laboratory. One day he noticed a blue-green growth in one of the

Left: Dr. Alexander Fleming

Below: Penicillin mold

cultures. It was in the center of the dish. Around this growth was a clear space. It looked as though germs could not grow in this space.

Dr. Fleming wondered if there was something in this blue-green mold that prevented bacteria growth. He grew more of the mold, which had already been named *penicillium*. After experimenting, he found that penicillium produced a chemical that prevented some germs from growing. It also killed other germs that had already grown. He called it *penicillin*.

How Could Penicillin be Removed from the Mold? Dr. Fleming had solved the problem of finding a substance to kill bacteria. But now he was faced with another problem that he could not solve. He could not remove penicillin from the mold. It was of no use to humans when it was embedded in the mold.

Dr. Howard Florey and Dr. Ernest Chain took up the problem where Dr. Fleming left off. Finally, they were able to obtain a small amount of penicillin. It was in the form of a white powder.

They used this powder in experiments with rats and proved that the drug would kill germs. Later, they used the drug with soldiers who had badly infected wounds. The results were very successful.

How Could Penicillin be Produced in Large Amounts? At first, penicillin was produced only in small amounts in laboratories. It was very expensive, and doctors could not get enough to meet their needs. In order to solve this problem, American drug companies began building huge tanks. In these tanks they placed a special broth in which the penicillium mold grows well. Now the drug companies can produce enough penicillin to supply the needs of all.

With the help of penicillin, millions of people throughout the world have recovered from diseases. Penicillin is used for pneumonia, boils, meningitis, diphtheria, and many other diseases.

ACTIVITY 1 — Problems, Solutions, Results

Use your own paper for this activity.

1. a. State Problem 1.
    b. What was done about it?
    c. What was the result?

2. a. State Problem 2.
    b. What was done about it?
    c. What was the result?

3. a. State Problem 3.
    b. What was done about it?
    c. What were the two results?
       (1)
       (2)

ACTIVITY 2 — Growing a Penicillium Mold

The pictures show the steps you would follow if you wanted to grow a penicillium mold. Study each picture and the text that goes with it.

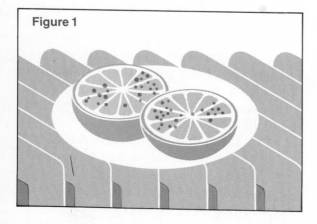

Figure 1. When a cut orange is put in a warm place and allowed to stand in the air, spores of molds that are floating in the air will settle on it.

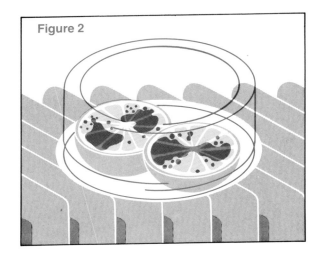

Figure 2. When the spore-covered orange is covered with a glass jar, the spores feed on the orange and begin to grow and form a mold.

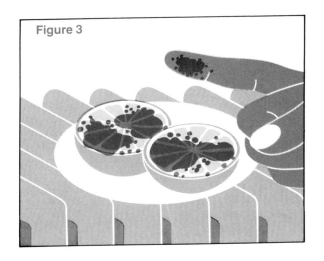

Figure 3. When you touch the blue-green penicillium mold with your finger, hundreds of tiny spores will stick to your finger or fly in the air.

3
ACTIVITY

A. Now that you know how a penicillium mold is grown, write on your paper the four steps you would follow in growing one yourself. (*Hint:* There are two steps combined in Figure 1.)

B. Answer the following questions:
  1. Why must the orange be left in the open air for a while?
  2. What do the spores feed on?
  3. What will you see on the orange after a short time?
  4. What is this called?
  5. What happens when you touch the mold with your finger?

47

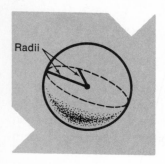

Radii

HOW TO READ IN MATHEMATICS

There is no doubt that you know the meaning of *circles* and *spheres* as these words are used in social studies. But do you know the exact meaning of *circles* and *spheres* as used in mathematics?

In working with this lesson you will have to read words, sentences, and diagrams. You will also have to do a lot of thinking and reasoning in order to answer questions about what you read. See how well you can read and understand the information given to you in the lesson that follows.

You have learned in social studies that only a small part of Alaska extends above the Arctic Circle. You have learned that the Arctic Circle is an imaginary line running around the earth parallel to the equator. You have read that the earth looks like a sphere and that half of the earth is called a *hemisphere*. You know that Alaska is in the Northern Hemisphere. This lesson will tell you the meaning of these words as you will meet them in studying in mathematics textbooks.

Describing Circles and Spheres _

Written for this book by William L. Schaaf.

Everyone knows what a circle is. It is a "ring"—a *closed curve* lying in a plane; every point in the curve is as far from a certain point (called the *center*) inside the circle as every other point in the curve.

The set of all points in the plane is made up of three distinct subsets: (1) the set of points *inside* the circle (called the interior); (2) the set of points *outside* the circle (called the exterior); and (3) the set of points making up the circle itself. The circle is a boundary between two regions in the plane. The points of the circle do not belong to either the interior or the exterior region. Remember that the word *circle* refers to a set of points, and not to the area enclosed by the circle.

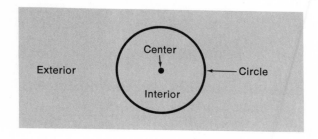

sphere (sfêr), a round object whose surface is at all points equally distant from the center.

infinitely (in′fə nit lē), without limits or bounds; very great; without end; of an endless number or amount.

We can think of a sphere in the same way. If we think of a balloon or a basketball filled with air, we can see that a sphere is a *closed surface* in space. Every point on the surface is as far from the center as every other point on the surface.

You can see that the set of all points in space is made up of three subsets: (1) the set of points *inside* the sphere; (2) the set of points *outside* the sphere; and (3) the set of points on the sphere itself. The sphere is the boundary between two regions in space. The points of the sphere belong neither to the interior nor the exterior region. Note that the word *sphere* refers to a set of points, not to the space enclosed by that set of points.

It is also helpful to describe *solid* objects such as a baseball, a billiard ball, or an orange as having the "shape of a sphere."

Properties of a Sphere

We can think of a straight line as an arrow. If a straight line (which is also a set of points) pierces a sphere once as it enters the sphere, it must pierce it again as it leaves the interior. In other words:

1. If a straight line intersects a sphere it has exactly two points in common with the sphere. (See Figure 1.)

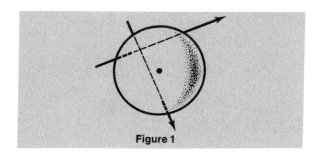

Figure 1

2. A line segment whose endpoints lie in a sphere and which passes through the center is called a *diameter* of the sphere. The distance from the center of the sphere to any point in the sphere is called a *radius*. (See Figure 2.)

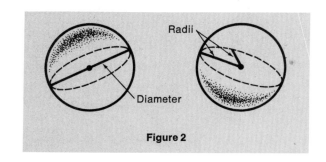

Figure 2

3. If a plane cuts a sphere, their intersection is always a circle. You can easily picture this if you think of slicing an apple with a knife. (See Figure 3.) You know from experience that the size of the circle will vary depending upon how close the cutting plane is to the center of the sphere. The cutting plane can take many different positions.

4. If a cutting plane passes through the center of the sphere, the circle formed is called a *great circle* of the sphere. The diameter of a great circle is equal to the diameter of the sphere. Infinitely many great circles exist in a sphere. (See Figure 4.)

5. If the cutting plane does not pass through the center of the sphere, the circle formed is called a *small circle* of the sphere. Infinitely many small circles can also exist in a sphere. (See Figure 5.)

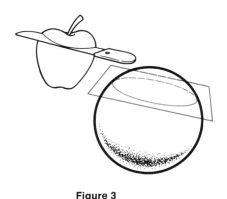

Figure 3

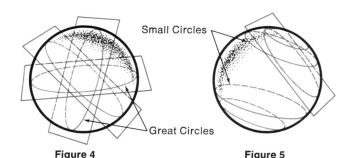

Figure 4   **Figure 5**

ACTIVITY 1

Understanding Circles in a Sphere

Read each statement below and on your paper write whether it is true (T) or false (F).

1. Some points in a sphere are nearer the center than other points in the sphere.

2. A sphere has infinitely many diameters.

3. The intersection of a plane and a sphere is an ellipse.

4. All the diameters of a sphere are equally long.

5. A diameter of a sphere is twice as long as a radius.

6. A straight line may intersect a sphere in three distinct points.

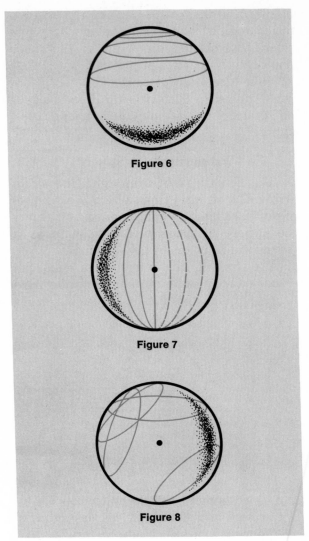

Figure 6

Figure 7

Figure 8

ACTIVITY 2

More About Spheres

1. Look at Figure 6 and then write whether the following are true or false:
   a. The nearer the cutting plane is to the center of a sphere, the smaller the circle of intersection will be.
   b. The planes of two small circles must always be parallel to each other.

2. Look at Figure 7 and answer the following:
   a. How many great circles can be drawn in a sphere?
   b. Are all great circles of a sphere equal?
   c. Must any two great circles of a sphere intersect each other?
   d. Do all great circles of a sphere cut each other exactly in half?

3. Look at Figure 8.
   a. How many small circles can be drawn through a given point in a sphere?
   b. Do all small circles of a given sphere have the same radius?
   c. Do any two small circles of a sphere have to intersect each other? May they intersect?

Finding Main Idea Sentences

You have already had some work in using the skill of finding the main idea in a paragraph. To become expert in using this skill, you need to have practice.

Remember to look for the sentence that is the "heart" of the paragraph. Sometimes it is the first sentence. Sometimes it is elsewhere in the paragraph.

Read the next selection. On your paper, write the sentence that contains the main idea of each paragraph.

Refrigeration

Written for this book
by Maurice U. Ames.

1. Human beings have learned several different ways of preserving food. In primitive days hunters had to kill animals practically every day in the warm season in order to have fresh meat. As the years went by, people learned to preserve meat by salting it and drying it in the sun. Pioneers cooked fruit and vegetables and canned them in airtight jars. Finally, it was discovered that food would stay fresh longer if it were kept in a cool cellar.

2. Refrigeration is an excellent way of preserving food. All methods of preserving food are based on the idea of killing bacteria or keeping bacteria from multiplying. Most bacteria cannot grow in low temperatures. So the cooling process known as refrigeration is used more generally than any other in preserving food at the present time.

3. Have you ever wondered why your wet skin feels cool as it dries in the air and your perspiring face feels cool when you fan it? Whenever a liquid changes to vapor (evaporates), there is a cooling effect.

4. All refrigerators depend upon the cooling effect of evaporation. A gas called *Freon* is the most commonly used gas in refrigerators. An electric motor, located at the bottom of the refrigerator, compresses the gas, making it hot. The hot compressed gas is passed through a condenser, where it is cooled. The cooled gas then condenses to a liquid. The liquid Freon is then pumped up into the upper part of the refrigerator. There, in the pipes of the freezing compartment, the liquid Freon evaporates. This evaporation absorbs heat from surrounding objects and produces the cooling effect in the upper pipes. Finally, the Freon in the form of a gas flows down to the motor, which again compresses it, beginning the cycle again.

---

refrigeration (ri frij′ēr ā′shən), the process of keeping food cool.

preserve (pri zērv′), to keep food from spoiling.

Freon (frē′on), a gas used to cool refrigerators.

compartment (kəm pärt′mənt), a separate division within an enclosed space.

Reviewing Silent Letters

Some words contain letters that have no sound when we pronounce the words. These letters are called *silent letters*. Consonants are sometimes silent, and vowels are sometimes silent.

You want to send the following telegraph messages, but each letter costs money. You decide to save money by leaving out silent letters. For the first message, you will leave out all the silent consonants in the underlined words. For the second message, you will leave out all the silent vowels in the underlined words.

On your paper, rewrite the underlined words, then cross out the silent consonants in the first message and the silent vowels in the second message.

A. Crossing Out Silent Consonants

I don't have time to (1) <u>write</u> you a (2) <u>letter</u> because this (3) <u>message</u> must reach you quickly. A (4) <u>corps</u> of killers may be after you. (5) <u>Follow</u> these instructions carefully.

(6) <u>Watch</u> for (7) <u>bombs</u>. (8) <u>Fasten</u> the (9) <u>latch</u> on your door at (10) <u>night</u> and don't (11) <u>answer</u> if someone (12) <u>knocks</u>. Don't eat anything, even a (13) <u>crumb</u>. (Your food may be poisoned.) Keep away from (14) <u>knives</u>, (15) <u>swords</u>, (16) <u>high</u> (17) <u>cliffs</u>, (18) <u>black</u> (19) <u>tunnels</u>, (20) <u>islands</u>, and (21) <u>ditches</u>. Keep your (22) <u>thigh</u> (23) <u>muscles</u> ready to run. Beware of everyone—even a (24) <u>calf</u>, (25) <u>lamb</u>, (26) <u>wren</u>, or (27) <u>gnat</u>. Don't do anything (28) <u>dumb</u>. As you (29) <u>know</u>, one (30) <u>wrong</u> move may be the end.

Don't (31) <u>discuss</u> this with anyone or make any (32) <u>sign</u>. Above all, don't (33) <u>dwell</u> on this (34) <u>solemn</u> news. Keep (35) <u>calm</u> and try not to (36) <u>worry</u>!

B. Crossing Out Silent Vowels

Did you (1) <u>receive</u> my first (2) <u>message</u>? It did (3) <u>contain</u> (4) <u>some</u> important instructions. More (5) <u>details</u> are now (6) <u>available</u>. Let me (7) <u>explain</u>. I have (8) <u>reason</u> to (9) <u>believe</u> that the (10) <u>people</u> who are after you plan to (11) <u>seize</u> their (12) <u>chance</u> soon. So (13) <u>increase</u> your (14) <u>guard</u> and (15) <u>glance</u> over your (16) <u>shoulder</u> at all (17) <u>times</u>. You should be safe as long as you (18) <u>remain</u> (19) <u>inside</u> and eat no (20) <u>meals</u>, not even a (21) <u>loaf</u> of (22) <u>bread</u>. On (23) <u>pain</u> of death, do not travel on a (24) <u>boat</u>, (25) <u>train</u>, or (26) <u>airplane</u>.

I'm sure you (27) <u>recognize</u> the fact that my (28) <u>goal</u> is to keep you (29) <u>alive</u> and well. So (30) <u>please</u> don't (31) <u>complain</u> about your lack of (32) <u>freedom</u>. Let me (33) <u>repeat</u>—by all (34) <u>means</u>, stay calm. You will (35) <u>laugh</u> about all this one (36) <u>day</u> (if by some miracle you're still around).

Reviewing Two-Letter Blends

When two consonants are blended together, this sound is called a *blend*. The most common two-letter blends are

bl, cl, fl, gl, pl, sl	br, cr, dr, fr, gr, pr, tr	sc, sk, sm, sn, sp, st, sw, tw

Check yourself to see how well you know these blends. Pronounce the word that each of the pictures represents. Then write the word on your paper and circle the blend.

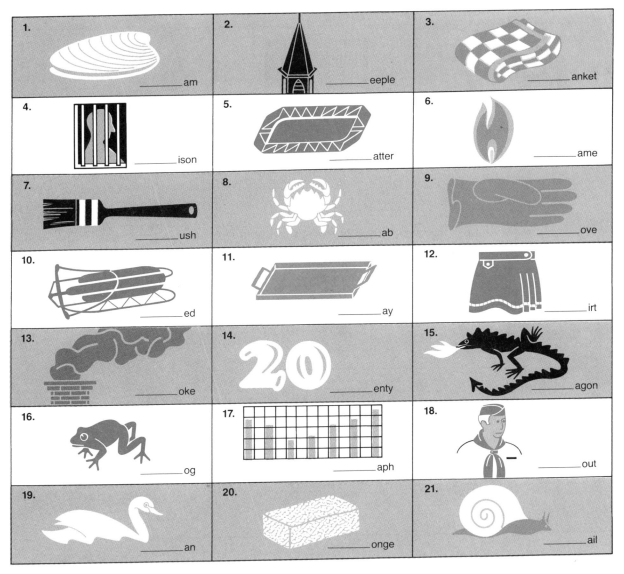

1. _____ am
2. _____ eeple
3. _____ anket
4. _____ ison
5. _____ atter
6. _____ ame
7. _____ ush
8. _____ ab
9. _____ ove
10. _____ ed
11. _____ ay
12. _____ irt
13. _____ oke
14. _____ enty
15. _____ agon
16. _____ og
17. _____ aph
18. _____ out
19. _____ an
20. _____ onge
21. _____ ail

Reviewing Three-Letter Blends and Digraphs

A. Words beginning with three-letter blends are more difficult to pronounce than words that begin with one consonant or a two-letter blend. These are the most common three-letter blends: *spr, str, shr, spl, scr, thr.*

On your paper write the three-letter combination to complete the word at the right of each picture.

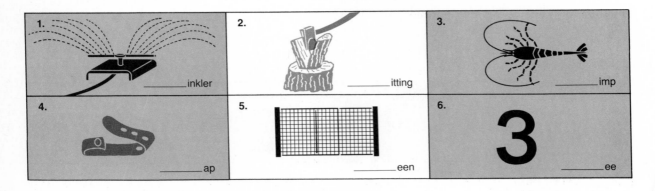

1. _____inkler
2. _____itting
3. _____imp
4. _____ap
5. _____een
6. _____ee

B. In the blends you can hear a little of each of the letters. In some consonant groups called digraphs you do not hear either of the two letters. The two letters combine to make a new sound entirely. The most common of these digraphs are: *sh, wh, ch, th,* and *ng.* The digraph *wh* never comes at the end of a word; however, *ng* always comes at the end of a word. *Sh, ch,* and *th* may come at the beginning or the end of a word.

See how well you know the sounds of these digraphs. On your paper write the digraph that completes the word for each of the pictures below.

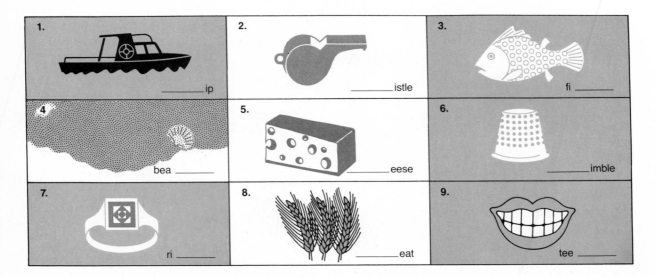

1. _____ip
2. _____istle
3. fi _____
4. bea _____
5. _____eese
6. _____imble
7. ri _____
8. _____eat
9. tee _____

Reviewing Vowel Sounds Changed by *r* _____

You reviewed the long and short sounds of the vowels in Unit 1 of this book. There are other sounds of vowels which you need to know.

When the letter *r* follows a vowel, it changes the sound of the vowel. The letter *r* changes the sound of *a* in two different ways. Sometimes *r* makes a sound as it does in ärm; at other times it makes a sound as it does in cãre. The sound of *a* as in cãre occurs in one-syllable words in which there are two vowels, as *share, bear, air.*

The letter *r* changes other vowels also. When *o* is followed by *r*, it makes the sound of *o* as in ôrb. The vowel *e* has a different sound when followed by *r* as in *term.* The vowels *i* and *u* often have this same sound when followed by *r* as in *bird* and *burn.* We use the symbol ũ to show this sound of *e, i,* or *u* followed by *r*. The pronunciation of *term* is shown in the dictionary like this: tũrm. The pronunciation of *bird* and *burn* are shown like this: bũrd and bũrn.

Below is a table showing the sounds of the different vowels. A sample word is given for each sound.

ā	age	ē	equal	ī	ice	ō	open	ū	use
a	hat	e	let	i	it	o	hot	u	cup
ä	arm	ẽ	over	ũ	bird	ô	fork	ũ	burn
ã	care	ê	here			ōō	food		
		ũ	term			oo	foot		
						oi	foil		
						ou	out		

In each group below, match each word in the left-hand column with its dictionary respelling in the right-hand column. Write the letter of the correct respelling on your paper.

A.

1. act	**a.** härd		
2. clock	**b.** shōot		
3. late	**c.** pil		
4. smile	**d.** smīl		
5. hard	**e.** stāj		
6. stage	**f.** skōol		
7. shoot	**g.** good		
8. else	**h.** klok		
9. school	**i.** rōz		
10. pill	**j.** akt		
11. rose	**k.** els		
12. good	**l.** lāt		

B.

1. short	**a.** tôrn
2. hunt	**b.** shãr
3. turn	**c.** mũl
4. prize	**d.** stũr
5. skit	**e.** hunt
6. torn	**f.** shũrt
7. mule	**g.** sũrv
8. fur	**h.** tũrn
9. stir	**i.** prīz
10. shirt	**j.** shôrt
11. serve	**k.** skit
12. share	**l.** fũr

Recognizing Word Parts

One of the best ways to improve your reading and your grades is to improve your methods of pronouncing new words and getting their meanings. The dictionary is, of course, the best place to look up word meanings. There are several other methods, however, which you can use.

1. Be sure to use the vocabulary aids that most of your textbooks give you.

2. Use the context. The rest of the sentence or paragraph often gives the meaning.

3. Take the time to pronounce a word that you don't recognize. Once you have broken it into syllables, you'll often find that you know the word after all. You already know the meanings of most of the bases, prefixes, and suffixes that are used to form long words. You can use this knowledge to get the meaning of a word. You will now be given practice in breaking words into parts.

A. Finding Base Words. Many words are made up of a base word together with one or more syllables which have been added at the beginning or end of the word. On your paper, write the base word in each of the words below. The first one is underlined for you.

1. <u>add</u>ition

2. activities

3. formation

4. discolor

5. successful

6. generally

7. classification

8. revisited

9. unthinking

10. nonprofit

11. disband

12. personal

B. Working with Prefixes and Suffixes. A word element placed before a base word to change its meaning is called a prefix. The prefix *re* means "again." The prefix *dis* means "not" or "apart."

A word element placed at the end of a word to change its meaning is called a suffix. The suffix *ion* means "act of." The suffix *ship* means "quality" or "skill." Thus, *leadership* means "skill in leading."

Some of the words in this story need a prefix or a suffix. Choose one of the prefixes or suffixes just mentioned for each numbered word. Write the new word on your paper and give its meaning. (Remember, you may need to drop a silent *e* when adding a suffix.)

The members of The Lakeshore Boys' Club were eating lunch when Ann burst in. "How dare you (1) ____<u>allow</u> girls in your club!" she said. "I (2) ____<u>approve</u> of any club that doesn't let girls in. It's (3) <u>discriminate</u> ____!"

"What do you mean?" I asked.

"You'd better (4) ____<u>read</u> the Constitution," Ann said. "(5) <u>Citizen</u> ____ in this country means equal rights for all!"

"All right!" I yelled. The whole (6) <u>discuss</u> ____ was not helping my (7) <u>digest</u> ____.

We decided to (8) ____<u>name</u> our club The Lakeshore Kids' Club.

I DON'T MIND HAVING GIRLS IN THE CLUB. I WAS JUST AFRAID TO SAY SO.

3

Fair Play

You probably remember that the events or actions that happen in a story are called the plot. Every plot can be divided into three parts: the beginning, the middle, and the end. The events that happen in the beginning usually set up the situation of the story and introduce the characters and conflict. The events in the middle move the story along and tell more about what happens to the characters. The end of the story tells how things turn out, what happens to the characters, and how the conflict is resolved — if it is.

As you read the next story, pay special attention to the plot. Think about the parts of a plot and try to notice when you are moving from one part into the next.

Record your beginning and ending times.

Have you ever been in a situation where you felt it was your fault that something awful happened to another person? How did you feel about it? How did it work out? In the next story, you will read about a boy to whom this happened. See if you can understand his feelings.

Storm on Owl's Head _____

Written for this book
by Glenn Munson.

Jack forced his legs forward, the narrow skis sinking deep into the newly fallen powder, the snow massing against his legs, forcing him to struggle for every inch of progress.

They had missed the old quarry road, the winding route taken earlier on their strenuous climb up the south slope of Owl's Head.

"We made it, Jack!" Andy had whooped, peeling off his gloves, holding out upturned palms for a victor's slap. "All right! First to reach Dorset Cave on cross-country skis. We'll make the *Guinness Book of World Records*, like that guy who ate 130 prunes in less than two minutes!"

But even then the snow was falling more heavily, the light breeze gathering into a chilling wind. The winter storm closed around them, swallowing the sound of their cheers.

Chief Wisner slammed the door shut against the swirling snow, stamping his boots on the rubber floor mat. He strode down the hall, crossed the squad room, and pushed into his office.

"We've got a truck jackknifed up on Bromley, cars stranded everywhere, two kids lost," he growled, "and I had to get stuck in a drift over by the diner."

He unzipped his jacket and sat behind the desk. "All we can do is twiddle our thumbs as long as this wind keeps up anyway," he grunted. "How do we stand?"

quarry (kwär′ē), a place where stone or slate is dug out.

Sergeant Price held a sheaf of papers. "Mrs. Tift's lined up 20 units from the Snowmobile Club, and Art Mooney over at the rescue squad's got a dozen pals coming in. You can figure 30 to 35 units can be at the Griswald farm with an hour's warning."

Chief Wisner nodded. "Call Albany?"

"Weather Bureau reports winds slowing down just west of Utica. They say it will be three hours before we're down to light breezes here."

The police chief glanced up at the clock and scowled. "Turning dark and we've got three hours to wait. They've already been out there long enough to die."

Jack's hands and feet throbbed with pain. Approaching darkness and the blizzard had shrunk visibility until he barely could make out the dark shadows of thick trees a few feet ahead.

He twisted around, but saw only swirling snow. Then a figure materialized from the whiteness. It lurched straight at Jack. Suddenly Andy was on him, his hands thudding against Jack's chest. "Where's the farm? Where is it?" Andy screamed.

Jack felt anger surging through him. He shoved hard against Andy, jarring him backwards. "What are you hitting me for? What's wrong with you?" he yelled.

"Your stupid idea." Andy sputtered. Then a sudden blast of driving wind made him gasp; his teeth chattered uncontrollably.

Jack's anger drained away as fast as it had come. He shivered, hearing Andy moan, "My foot hurts so bad, Jack."

Maybe finding the quarry road didn't even matter anymore. Jack shuddered, forcing the idea from his mind.

He could just see Andy, doubled over, trying to warm his hands. "It can't be much farther, Andy. I'm pretty sure the trail's just down to our right. Come on." He bent forward and pushed off, breaking a slow path through the darkened woods.

The snowmobiles' whine was muffled by the falling snow. Once across the Griswald fields they would divide and fan out in three groups to draw a network of search patterns over the slopes of Owl's Head.

Only the idling engine and crackly static of the CB receiver broke the silence in the squad car. Chief Wisner stared out at the snow, tinted blue, then red, by the pulsing dome lights of the two squad cars and the rescue squad ambulance. All he could do now was wait. He sighed, thinking of the slim chance of the kids' surviving.

How long had it been dark, two hours, three, six? It seemed to Jack they'd been staggering through the deep snow forever, plodding step after endless step. His whole body was numb, and he moved as if in a dream. Moving on foot was scarcely easier than on the abandoned skis, but it let Jack keep closer to Andy.

Andy was in bad shape. His eyes were dazed now, his expression blank. He stumbled and fell often, and Jack had to bully him and plead with him and yank him to his feet, forcing him to go on.

"Come on, Andy, just a little more," and he grabbed for Andy's hand.

"Hey, what happened to your gloves, Andy?" The boy stared vacantly into the darkness. "Where are your gloves?" Jack yelled. Andy looked dully at his bare hands. "Let's stop and rest," he mumbled. "Okay? Feel a lot warmer now," Andy shivered violently. "Fingers hardly ache any more. Just lemme rest a little."

Doctor Hadley and two people from the rescue squad were wrapping the unconscious boy in blankets in the ambulance when a snowmobile rumbled up. Before it came to a stop, Jack jumped out and ran to the ambulance. He burst into wild sobs.

"I couldn't help it. I tried to make him get up, I tried to make him keep going—"

"Shut up!" Chief Wisner's voice was like a slap.

"My fault . . . but I couldn't make him move—"

"Stop it, Jack!" Chief Wisner shouted, his hands gripping the boy's shoulders, shaking him violently. "Shut up! Stop it!"

The boy tried to pull away from the police chief.

"Not your fault! Not your fault, Jack!" Chief Wisner yelled, still shaking the boy. "You did all you could; no one's blaming you!"

With Andy settled in the ambulance, Doctor Hadley stepped quickly between Jack and the police chief. She called brisk instructions to the men as she helped Jack into the ambulance.

The doctor turned to Chief Wisner. "Don't know about frostbite till I examine him, but this one looks as if he'll be okay," she said.

Chief Wisner's face was tight with strain. "And Andy? How about Andy?"

Doctor Hadley looked steadily at her friend. "Bad frostbite of his fingers and toes," she said, "and his temperature's dropped."

There was silence. Then the doctor spoke again. "These sudden storms can be killers, Ben, but your boy will pull through. We got to them just in time. Another half hour and it would have been a different story."

1
ACTIVITY

Fact Questions

1. What was Andy and Jack's goal?

2. What happened that they hadn't counted on?

3. How does Chief Wisner describe the situation?

4. What preparations are being made to rescue the boys?

5. How long will it be before the wind slows down?

6. In what way does Andy first act strange?

7. What does Chief Wisner fear might happen to the boys?

8. How does Andy's behavior change?

9. What does Chief Wisner do to Jack when the boys are brought to the ambulance?

10. What is Andy's relationship to Chief Wisner?

Copy this chart on your paper. Compute and record your WPM as you did on page 28.

Give yourself a score of 10 for each correct answer in Activity 1. This is your comprehension score. Record it on the chart.

	Hr.	Min.	Sec.
Ending time:	_____	_____	_____
Beginning time:	_____	_____	_____
Total Time:	_____	_____	_____

No. words:
No. seconds: $\left(\dfrac{1052}{}\right) \times 60 =$ _____ **WPM**

Comprehension Score: _____

ACTIVITY 2 Thought Questions

1. What stages do Jack's feelings go through?

2. What happens to Andy's spirit?

3. What causes him to change in this way?

4. What impression do you have of Chief Wisner in the beginning of the story?

5. What might Chief Wisner be feeling when he confronts Jack at the ambulance?

6. What might Jack be feeling?

7. Why do you think Chief Wisner says "No one's blaming you"?

ACTIVITY 3 Thinking About Plot

Number your paper from 1 to 10. Read each statement below and decide in what part of the story each happened. Then write *B* for beginning, *M* for middle, or *E* for end. Use these hints to help you decide:

Beginning—sets up the situation, introduces the characters, introduces the conflict or problem.

Middle—moves the story along and tells more about what happens to the characters.

End—tells how things turn out, what happens to the characters, and how the conflict is resolved.

1. Darkness makes it hard to see.

2. The rescue squad finds the boys.

3. Jack and Andy miss the road.

4. Andy's hands become numb.

5. Andy is put into the ambulance.

6. The police become worried about the boys.

7. Andy lunges at Jack.

8. The blizzard begins.

9. Jack blames himself for what happens to Andy.

10. A search party is formed.

Many of the things you will read about in social studies will be things that you are already familiar with. When you read such material, think about things in your own experience that are similar to what you are reading about.

As you read the next selection, think about similar situations or experiences that you know about. Think about how reading material like this can make you more aware and help you in your own life.

**HOW TO READ IN
SOCIAL STUDIES**

Women in Sports

Written for this book
by Sheila Burns.

A girl of ten sat unhappily at the breakfast table. She had just been told not to play football anymore because it wasn't ladylike.

"What can I play?" she asked her father.

He thought for a while. "Golf, swimming, or tennis," he answered.

"What's tennis?" she asked, and her father explained.

Years later, after the little girl had grown up, she recalled that day at the breakfast table. "I realize now," she said, "that my potential athletic career got chopped in half right then." That little girl succeeded in sports anyway, for she is Billie Jean King, the famous tennis champion.

As a child, Billie Jean accepted what she was told by her father. Years later she realized that she had been excluded from many sports. Perhaps she had physical talents that were never used. Perhaps she could have been a champion in another game besides tennis. In any case, doors had been closed to her. Because she was a girl, she had not been allowed to play some of the sports she enjoyed.

In the past if girls tried to participate in sports, they faced difficulties. In one case, a female track coach joined the faculty of a college and was given a budget of $900 to handle the team. "What is the boys' budget?" she asked. It was $9,000. The coach could see that the college did not consider the girls' athletic competition very important.

Often the girls' teams have not received very good coaching. Since many women coaches were never encouraged to compete themselves, they are not well-equipped to help others. Sometimes, when girls take part in athletic events, they must wait until the boys' teams have finished to use the court or the field.

If girls want financial support to help them train, they find little help from anyone. Many boys receive athletic scholarships to college. They are given payments for their expenses so that they can train and develop themselves. In professional sports men have been paid far more than women. Salaries and prize money have been much greater for male athletes.

Sportswriters devote nearly all their space to describing the male events. When women participate in athletics, newspapers do not report the events in much detail. Female winners are given a few lines at the bottom of the page.

In addition, many women athletes dislike the kinds of stories that are written

about them and the kinds of questions reporters ask. Often the reporters have far more to say about a woman's attractiveness than about her skills. Women who have trained every day for years are upset at this kind of reporting. They have worked hard and deserve respect for their athletic abilities, but they have not received that respect.

Fortunately, attitudes are changing. People are speaking out to tell girls the truth about athletics. A doctor, using research, showed that exercise will not necessarily give a woman bulging muscles. During seven months of weight lifting, the women in the test increased their strength by about 30 percent, but their muscle size increased only slightly. At the same time, the men in the survey gained almost twice as much in muscle size.

Other studies show that the female athlete is healthier than many other women. She is not a tomboy who never grew up. On the contrary, the woman athlete has confidence and assurance. She is strong mentally as well as physically.

Because attitudes are changing, women are trying new sports. They are organizing football teams, riding in rodeos, and playing ice hockey. They are finding better facilities at both amateur and professional levels. Even prize money is increasing. And every day, women are breaking their own athletic records while increasing their physical achievements.

There is a popular saying, "You've come a long way, baby." In sports, that saying is certainly true. There's still a long way to go in women's athletics, but it's beginning to look not quite so far anymore.

1 ACTIVITY

Approval from others can help an athlete perform well; disapproval can harm performance. Suppose a woman athlete hears the following remarks before going into a game or a meet. Which would help her?

Write the numbers of the following remarks on your paper. Write *help* after the number of each encouraging remark, *harm* after each discouraging one.

1. "Don't get a sunburn for the party tonight."

2. "Your weight is better today than it ever has been."

3. "I worry when I see you get so red in the face. Isn't it bad for you?"

4. "So what if you lose? Who cares?"

5. "I am so proud of you. I'm glad we have a winner in the family."

6. "Is this game going to take all afternoon? I hate to wait around for you."

7. "You just think about winning. I'll do your chores around the house for the next few weeks while you work out."

8. "Wouldn't you rather be a cheerleader for the boys' team?"

**HOW TO READ IN
SCIENCE**

This selection is similar to material you often find in your science books. As you have already been told, you should read such material differently from the way you read a story or social studies material.

Scientists often experiment with or observe some general group of things until they can divide the larger group into smaller groups. Each of the smaller groups is different in some ways from the others. This is called the *classification method.*

The selection below is a classification article about some of the important vitamins. The main headings tell you what the general classifications are. The subheadings name the smaller classifications.

1. Glance through the entire selection to find the names of the different groups of vitamins, both the major groups and the subgroups.
2. Read to find out (a) the uses of each vitamin; and (b) where each vitamin is found.

Suppose you are working out to be as fit as you can for a big athletic competition. Your coach will help you with exercises, and you know you must have enough rest and sleep. But what should you eat to be at your best? Read the following article to find out.

Vitamins

You will remember that proper amounts of proteins, fats, carbohydrates, and minerals are necessary in everyone's diet. In addition, certain chemicals found in foods are necessary to help us grow and to keep us healthy. These chemicals are called vitamins. Since the 1920's scientists have discovered many vitamins and feel that there are still more to be found.

Vitamins were labeled with letters of the alphabet. Thus, we have vitamins B_1, B_2, B_6, B_{12}, C, D, and K. Some vitamins now are generally known by their chemical names rather than by their letters. Vitamin B_1 is thiamine, B_2 is riboflavin, and C is ascorbic acid. Another B vitamin is called niacin.

---

thiamine (thī′ə min), another name for vitamin B_1.

riboflavin (rī bə flā′vən), another name for vitamin B_2.

ascorbic acid (askôr′bik as′id), another name for vitamin C.

niacin (nī′ə sin), one of the B vitamins.

margarine (mär′jə rin), a fat used in place of butter.

beriberi (ber′ē ber′ē), a disease caused by lack of vitamins.

convulsion (kən vul′shən), a violent contracting and relaxing of the muscles, a spasm.

pellagra (pə lā′grə), a disease affecting the nerves, caused by a lack of niacin.

rickets (rik′its), a disease marked by softening of the bones.

irradiate (i rā′dē āt′), treat by exposing to ultraviolet rays.

Vitamin A

Vitamin A helps us grow. It is very necessary for the health of the eyes and it keeps the skin healthy. Milk and butter will provide you with a good amount of vitamin A, as will enriched margarine. This vitamin is found in green and yellow vegetables and also in fruits. The yellow vegetables and fruits are especially rich in vitamin A. Fish liver oils, egg yolks, and meats like kidney, liver, and heart all contain vitamin A.

The B Vitamins

Vitamin B_1, or thiamine. Vitamin B_1 was one of the first vitamins found. Chinese and Japanese soldiers often suffered from a disease called *beriberi*. They lived almost entirely on polished rice. A doctor found that when the men were fed whole-grain rice with meat and vegetables, they didn't get beriberi. The search began for the chemical that prevented beriberi, and vitamin B_1 was found.

It was later learned that B_1 has other uses. It gives one a good appetite, helps digestion, and aids the body in using carbohydrates.

Vitamin B_2, or riboflavin. Vitamin B_2 keeps the skin and muscles healthy. Most important of all, it helps the body change

foods into energy. Meats, dairy products, and green vegetables contain vitamin B_2.

Vitamin B_6. Scientists are still studying the uses of this vitamin. They believe that the lack of it may cause some skin diseases in adults and convulsions in babies. This vitamin is found in the same foods in which thiamine and riboflavin are found.

Vitamin B_{12}. This is the latest of the B vitamins to be discovered. This vitamin aids growth by giving us a good appetite. It also helps to build red blood cells. B_{12} is found in milk, eggs, liver, and meat.

Niacin. The most important use of this vitamin is to prevent a disease called *pellagra*. It is known also to aid growth and to help the stomach and intestines to work properly. Lean meat, fish, and liver contain niacin.

Vitamin C

This vitamin, known as *ascorbic acid*, is needed for good teeth and healthy gums. It also prevents scurvy. Vitamin C is found in oranges, grapefruit, lemons, limes, tomatoes, strawberries, and cabbage.

Vitamin D

Vitamin D is one of the most important vitamins. This vitamin helps to build strong bones and teeth and also helps to prevent rickets.

We get this vitamin from sunshine. Other sources are fish oils, egg yolks, and irradiated milk. This is milk which has been bathed in certain light rays. It is labeled "vitamin D" milk.

Vitamin K

One more vitamin you should be familiar with is vitamin K. This vitamin helps the blood to clot, and thus is an aid in stopping the flow of blood in case of cuts or wounds. It is found in leafy green vegetables, egg yolks, and milk.

1 ACTIVITY Classifying Vitamins

Copy these headings onto your paper. Then write the name of each vitamin, give one or two important uses, and name one or two sources of each vitamin.

Name	Uses	Where Found

HOW TO READ IN MATHEMATICS

In doing the work on these two pages you will have practice in reading common fractions, decimal fractions, and decimals expressed in numerals. All of this is just like reading words, only in this case you will be reading mathematical symbols.

No doubt you have basketball and baseball at your school.

In addition to playing games, you watch games and read about games played by others. As you watch a game or read about a game, can you always tell exactly what the scores mean? Understanding common fractions, decimal fractions, decimals, and averages will help in giving you a better understanding of scores.

Fractions and Decimals

Written for this book by William L. Schaaf.

A baseball team played 12 games and won 8 of them. What fractional part of the games played did they win? We say: 8 out of $12 = \frac{8}{12} = \frac{2}{3}$. How do we know that $\frac{8}{12} = \frac{2}{3}$?

$$\frac{8}{12} = \frac{2 \times 4}{3 \times 4} = \frac{2}{3} \times \frac{4}{4} = \frac{2}{3} \times 1 = \frac{2}{3}$$

At darts, a player made 6 bull's-eyes out of 24 throws. What fraction of the throws were bull's-eyes?

$$\frac{6}{24} = \frac{6 \times 1}{6 \times 4} = \frac{6}{6} \times \frac{1}{4} = 1 \times \frac{1}{4} = \frac{1}{4}$$

When we change a fraction in this way, we are finding its simplest form.

1 ACTIVITY

Write on your paper the simplest form of each of the following fractions:

1. $\frac{3}{9}$ 3. $\frac{4}{12}$ 5. $\frac{6}{8}$ 7. $\frac{10}{15}$

2. $\frac{5}{20}$ 4. $\frac{8}{10}$ 6. $\frac{12}{16}$ 8. $\frac{7}{21}$

Any common fraction such as $\frac{1}{5}, \frac{3}{4}$, or $\frac{5}{8}$ can also be written as a *decimal fraction*.

YOU'RE A FRACTION OF YOUR OLD SELF.

Since a fraction such as $\frac{1}{5}$ means "$1 \div 5$," we simply divide:

$$5\overline{)1.0}^{\,.2} \qquad 4\overline{)3.00}^{\,.75} \qquad 8\overline{)5.000}^{\,.625}$$

To show that .2 means $\frac{1}{5}$, we think:

.2 means $\frac{2}{10}$; and $\frac{2}{10} = \frac{1}{5}$,

since $2 \times 5 = 10 \times 1$.

In the same way:

.75 means $\frac{75}{100}$; and $\frac{75}{100} = \frac{3}{4}$, since

$$75 \times 4 = 100 \times 3.$$

.625 means $\frac{625}{1000}$; and $\frac{625}{1000} = \frac{5}{8}$, since

$$625 \times 8 = 1000 \times 5.$$

ACTIVITY 2

On your paper, change each of these common fractions to decimal fractions:

1. $\frac{1}{4}$ 3. $\frac{4}{5}$ 5. $\frac{7}{10}$ 7. $\frac{3}{8}$ 9. $\frac{3}{25}$

2. $\frac{3}{5}$ 4. $\frac{1}{2}$ 6. $\frac{7}{20}$ 8. $\frac{3}{50}$ 10. $\frac{4}{16}$

Sometimes the division does not "come out even," which means that there is a remainder. When this happens, we can stop the division at any place we wish, and *round* the result. For example:

a. Write $\frac{2}{3}$ as a decimal fraction to two decimal places.

$3\overline{)2.00}^{\,.66\ R2}$; and $.66\frac{2}{3}$ is .67, to the nearest hundredth.

b. Write $\frac{6}{11}$ as a decimal fraction to three decimal places.

$11\overline{)6.000}^{\,.545\ R5}$; and $.545\frac{5}{11}$ is .545, to the nearest thousandth.

ACTIVITY 3

On your paper, write as decimal fractions, rounding to the nearest thousandth:

1. $\frac{1}{3}$ 2. $\frac{5}{9}$ 3. $\frac{5}{6}$ 4. $\frac{2}{7}$

Baseball averages are often written as 3-place decimals. If a ballplayer made 15 hits in 46 official times at bat, what was the batting average? The average number of hits is $\frac{15}{46}$, or

$$46\overline{)15.000}^{\,.326} \text{ (Batting Average)}$$

5. In 245 times at bat, a player scored 83 hits. Find the batting average.

6. In one season, a well-known Yankee player made 188 hits. He went to bat 533 times. What was his average that season?

7. Team averages are also written as decimals. A team won 105 games out of 167. What was the team's average?

71

Reading and Organizing Details

You have had practice in finding the main idea in paragraphs. In some cases finding this large basic idea will serve your purpose. In much of your studying, however, you need to grasp and understand details. Reading for details is more difficult than reading for main ideas. There are ways, however, of learning to grasp details easily and quickly.

The first step to take in finding details in a paragraph is to find the main idea. The smaller ideas, or details, grow out of the main idea and tell about it. Once you get a "picture" of smaller ideas growing out of a main idea, it is easy to grasp these smaller ideas, or details.

There are two kinds of details. There are *major* details and *minor* details. The major details in a paragraph are of about equal importance. Minor details grow out of major details and are less important. Minor details give information about major details.

First you will have practice in working with major details. Diagramming a paragraph is often helpful in getting a "picture" of a main idea and its major details. You will now be shown how to diagram a paragraph. Read the following paragraph quickly and see if you can find the main idea.

Death Valley became world-famous for its unlimited stores of borax. The borax occurs in beds, partly beneath the earth's surface, varying in thickness from a few inches to a hundred feet. It was mined from these beds by means of shafts and tunnels. For many years this product of the mines was hauled out of the valley by long trains of mules. The mules became obsolete. Then a narrow-gauge railroad started hauling out the ore.

No doubt you discovered at once that the main idea is "Death Valley became world-famous for its unlimited stores of borax."

Now find several details of about equal importance that tell more about this main idea.

Think of this whole set of details together with the main idea as making one cluster of ideas. Perhaps this block diagram will help you to "picture" the entire paragraph.

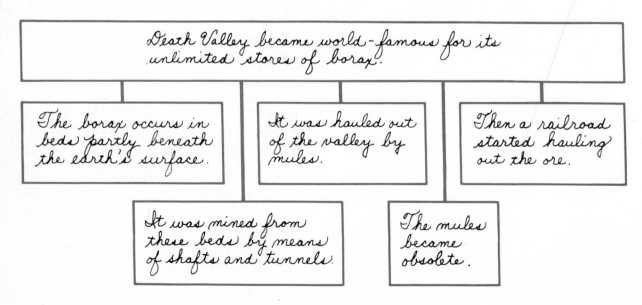

In making a block diagram, you don't have to write every word in the main idea sentence or in the detailed sentences. Compare the sentences in the block diagram with the sentences in the paragraph. Notice that only the important words and phrases are written in the blocks.

Here are some additional paragraphs. Use your own paper and make block diagrams for these paragraphs. Write only the most important words of a sentence in each block.

A Valley of Death and Prosperity[1]

1. Death Valley is a famous valley in southern California. It earned its sinister name in the middle of the nineteenth century. At that time an emigrant party went astray in its dreary wastes. Most of the members perished miserably of thirst. Since then Death Valley has long been a center of activity and a source of great wealth. Vast mineral resources once created a mining industry, and a tourist industry gives the valley its present prosperity.

2. Death Valley is the lowest bit of dry land in America. Nearly all of it lies below sea level. It has an extreme depth of about four hundred feet. This is all the more remarkable because of the high mountains which border the valley. One of these mountains rises nearly 11,000 feet above sea level. Only eighty miles away is Mount Whitney, with an altitude of 14,500 feet.

3. In summer, Death Valley is perhaps the hottest, driest spot on earth. Periods of six consecutive months without rain are not uncommon. A day without sunshine is almost unheard of. The air is not generally stagnant but is stirred by hot blasts. These cause wonderful mirages in the desert. Whirling dust storms are often caused by hot blasts, also.

[1] Numbered footnote references can be found on page iv.

---

stagnant (stag′nənt), without motion, not flowing.
mirage (mi räzh′), an optical illusion caused by reflection of light through layers of air of different temperatures.

4. Today the valley is a popular tourist attraction. There are ghost towns, ruins of borax mills, wonderful views, even desert flowers. Several hotels have been built. "Death Valley Scotty's" Castle, a mysterious mansion in the desert, is of particular interest to tourists.

73

Outlining Paragraphs That Have Major Details ___

In working with the last four paragraphs, you searched for the main idea and major details. You showed how major details are related to the main idea by making and filling in block diagrams. You can also show how major details are related to a main idea by outlining a paragraph. Now you will have practice in outlining paragraphs. Your first step is to find the main idea. Your second step is to find the details that tell about this main idea.

Read the paragraph below to find the main idea, and then to find the major details that go with it. The main idea and major details are shown in the outline.

Many things happen to raw hides before they can be made into shoes. First the hide of the animal is removed and sent to a tannery. Here it is soaked in water to soften and clean it. Then the hide is soaked again in a solution of lime to loosen the hair. The hair is then removed by scraping machines.

Main Idea:	Details:
1. Many things happen to raw hides before they can be made into shoes.	A. Hide removed, sent to tannery
	B. Soaked in water to soften and clean
	C. Soaked in lime to loosen hairs
	D. Hair removed by scraping machines

Read the following article to find the main idea and major details in each numbered paragraph. After reading each paragraph, make an outline to show the main idea and major details for that paragraph. Do not write all the words in each sentence. Just take out the important part and write that. Use your own paper for your outlines, and follow the form shown here. Work only with the numbered paragraphs.

◤ Rules for a Good Sport

If a person is a good sport, teammates, competitors, and spectators at the sporting event notice it at once. Even if players lose the game, they are approved of if they are good sports. Even if they win the game, they are disapproved of if they are poor sports.

Being a good sport is just as important in everything we do in life as it is in games and sports. Our friends, our families, and our fellow workers approve of us if we are good sports, and disapprove if we are poor sports.

Here are some rules to help you be a good sport.

1. **Show consideration for others.** When you have an unpleasant job to do, remember it is also unpleasant for others. Don't pity yourself or try to get someone else to do it for you. Go ahead with your difficult, dull tasks and help others when they are doing an unpleasant task. Follow the golden rule of doing for others as you would have them do for you, and then you can be sure that you are showing consideration.

2. **Follow the rules of the game.** In playing a game, there are certain rules that all must follow in order that the game be played fairly. If someone doesn't follow these rules, that person is not allowed to continue playing. There are rules for

---

consideration (kən sid′ə rā′shən), thoughtfulness of others.

74

doing many other things in life too. There are rules for doing your school work, crossing the street, participating in fire drills, driving a car, picking wild flowers in certain places, putting out campfires, and many other things. These rules are made not only for your own good, but also for the good of others. It is just as important that you follow these rules as it is for the football player to follow the rules in a football game.

3. **Work with the team.** Even though you are not always playing a game, you are nearly always working or playing with a kind of team. Your class in school is a team; a committee which is asked to do a certain thing in the classroom is a team. The group of friends with whom you spend much time outside of school is a team. Your family is a team. Usually, each group has a certain goal or goals. It is your job to support the "team" in every way you can to help it reach its goals.

4. **Be a good loser.** One of the important ways to be a good sport is to take disappointment, defeat, or bad luck with a smile. Then start trying harder than ever to do better next time. A good loser never complains, makes excuses, sulks, or hits back with words when he fails at something. Doing any of these things can bring no good to anyone. They are often harmful to the loser. The thing to do is to clear your mind of the old disappointment and give all of your thought and energy to new goals ahead.

Dividing Words into Syllables

You are beginning to read material in your grade in which there are many long words—words of three, four, or five syllables. These long words are the ones that students most often have trouble in pronouncing. You have reviewed the sounds of letters and letter combinations. Now you will review some quick ways to break a word into syllables. Then you should be able to pronounce any word, long or short, that you meet.

What is a syllable? You have already learned that a syllable is a word or a part of a word in which there is a *sounded* vowel. Silent vowels don't count when dividing words into syllables.

You know how to tell when a vowel is silent; when two vowels come together in a word, one of them is usually silent; also, when a single vowel is followed by a final *e*, the final *e* is usually silent. With these two thoughts in mind decide how many *sounded* vowels are in each word. This will tell you the number of syllables. Finding syllables is the first thing to do when learning to pronounce long words.

On your paper, make five columns numbered from 1 to 5. Sort each of the words below and copy it onto your paper under the column that tells how many syllables are heard in each word. The following will show you how to place the words:

When you copy the numbered words below, be sure to copy the letter in front of each word along with the word so you can find the hidden message.

1. I. danger
2. W. main
3. H. twins
4. N. total
5. D. divide
6. E. branch
7. O. explain

8. T. vitamin
9. R. important
10. E. historical
11. G. imaginary
12. S. continental
13. Y. consonant
14. N. space
15. U. control

16. G. telephone
17. B. complete
18. S independence
19. T. children
20. U. newspaper
21. I. carbohydrate
22. N. information

Guides for Dividing Words into Syllables

A. Guide 1: Dividing Between Words Forming Compounds. There are several guides that you can use to divide a word into syllables. One of the easiest guides is the one that can be used with compound words. You can always divide compound words between the words that form the compound word. Sometimes one, or perhaps two, of the words forming a compound word are made up of more than one syllable; but you are always safe in dividing between the two words as a starting point. On your paper, divide these compound words. The first one is done for you.

1. bakeshop *bake shop*
2. horseback
3. airport
4. watchman
5. earthquake
6. withdrawn
7. halfway
8. northwest
9. runway

B. Guide 2: Dividing Between Double Consonants. Another easy guide is one that works with double-consonant words. When a word has double consonants (*dd, ss,* etc.) within it, you usually break it into syllables by dividing between the double consonants. On your paper, divide the words below into syllables.

1. message
2. getting
3. coffee
4. current
5. carry
6. pollen
7. correct
8. support

C. Guide 3: Dividing Between Separately Sounded Consonants. When two separately sounded consonants come between two sounded vowels in a word, you usually break it into syllables by dividing between the consonants. The word *basket,* for instance, has two separately sounded consonants, *s* and *k,* between two sounded vowels, *a* and *e.* So you divide between the *s* and the *k*: *bas ket.* On your paper, divide the words below, using Guide 3.

1. center
2. perhaps
3. order
4. absorb
5. certain
6. Neptune
7. fancy
8. condense

D. Guide 4: Dividing When There Is a Single Consonant. When a word contains a single consonant between two sounded vowels, you usually break it into syllables by dividing (a) just *after* the consonant if the first vowel is short, and (b) just *before* the consonant if the first vowel is long or if it has a sound that is neither long nor short. The word *vital,* for instance, has a single consonant, *t,* between two sounded vowels. Since the first vowel is long, you divide before the *t: vi tal.* The word *camel* also has one consonant between two sounded vowels. The first vowel is short, so you divide it: *cam el.* On your paper, divide the words below, using Guide 4.

1. famous
2. proceed
3. climate
4. total
5. limit
6. taper
7. modern
8. locate
9. credit
10. chorus
11. human
12. glory

77

Critical Reading: What Do Those Words *Really* Tell You?

In this unit, you have read about the nutritional value of certain food groups. You learned how vitamins and minerals help to keep you healthy and fit. But when you buy a new breakfast cereal, for instance, how much attention do you pay to the nutritional value? Many people pay more attention to the things they have read in an ad or heard on a TV commercial.

Every year advertisers spend billions of dollars trying to get you to buy their products rather than others. Advertisers use expressions like *fortified, vitamin enriched, richest tasting,* and *freshest smelling,* to make their products attractive. As a consumer, you should figure out what these terms really mean and what the advertiser may *not* be telling you.

Activity 1

Number your paper from 1 to 5. Read each of the numbered advertising claims. Next to that number on your paper, write the letter of the question that you should have answers for before you decide to buy the product. (Some of the claims will have more than one question to answer.)

A. What is an average serving?
B. What vitamins (and/or minerals)?
C. What other things might have been added to it?

1. Start your day with All-Day, the vitamin-enriched breakfast cereal.

2. Blast-Off, the drink of the space travelers, gets your kids' day off to the right start. Just one glass is full of the vitamins and minerals kids need.

3. Lose weight and stay healthy at the same time. Drink Skinny Slurp, the meal in a glass that satisfies the minimum daily need of essential vitamins, minerals, and protein without adding needless calories.

4. For that afternoon lag, try KwikSnak, the munchy treat that adds to your nutritional needs.

5. DeliSlice tastes delicious and stays fresher twice as long as most other breads.

THEY CALL THIS AN AVERAGE SERVING?

Working with Mathematics Words and Phrases

The words and phrases below appear in mathematics textbooks at your level. Work out the pronunciation of each of the words or phrases. Pronounce the word or phrase distinctly to yourself. Then study the meaning which each word has in mathematics.

---

broker (brō′kĕr), one who brings together buyers and sellers and receives a sum for the sales contract.

commission (kə mish′ən), the percentage of the total amount of a sale that is paid to a broker.

decimal system (des′ə ml sis′təm), a system of measurement or coinage that is based upon units of ten.

installment plan (in stôl′mənt plan), a way to buy goods by paying for them in small amounts over a period of time.

metric system (met′rik sis′təm), a decimal system of weights and measures that is based on the meter (about $39\frac{1}{2}$ inches long).

mill (mil), one tenth of a cent in United States money. It is not actually a coin; the mill is only used in figuring.

pence (pens), the British plural for penny; 5 pennies would be called "5 pence."

penny (pen′ē), a coin equal to $\frac{1}{100}$ of a pound in the new British money system. Under the old system, there were 240 pence to the pound, and each penny was worth about one cent in United States money.

pound (pound), a British unit of money that was equal to 20 shillings or 240 pence. Under the new money system, the pound is equal to 100 British pence.

shilling (shil′iŋ), a British silver coin of the old system that was equal to 12 pence.

See if you know the meaning of each of these words as it is used in mathematics. On your paper, write the word that fits in each blank space. Add *s* if necessary.

1. Mr. Ricardo paid $100 per month on his car. He bought it on the _____.

2. In countries using the _____ _____ distances are measured in meters.

3. Mr. Klein wanted a new home, but he did not know where there were houses for sale. He required the services of a _____.

4. The man who helped Mr. Klein find and make arrangements for buying a new house received a _____ of $500.

5. Tom had 12 British pence. Under the old system, what British coin could he have gotten in exchange for his pence? _____.

6. Bill bought a sweater in Great Britain which cost 40 shillings. Under the old system, what British unit of money could he have used in place of the shillings? _____. How many? _____.

7. Under the old system, what part of a British shilling was a British penny? _____.

8. Jack paid one shilling and 7 pence for some candy. How many pence did he pay for the candy? _____.

9. A unit of money which is worth $\frac{1}{100}$ of a dime is called a _____. If a person should ask for ten of these, would he get them? _____.

10. A money system based on units of ten is a _____.

4

The Struggle
For Independence

When you are reading a story, it is important to know when and where the events take place. The time and place of a story are called the *setting.* Some authors tell you about the setting directly, like this:

A. In the hot July of 1863, the Battle of Gettysburg raged for a third day.

Other authors may simply hint at the setting as they describe the actions or feelings of a character, like this:

B. Aaron felt the sun beating on his body and the sweat streaming down his face as he lay in the hills of western Pennsylvania praying the Rebel scouts wouldn't find him.

If you compare the two sentences on the chart below, you will see that the information both give is much the same:

	Stated in A	Suggested in B
weather	hot	hot (sun beating, sweat pouring)
time of year	July	summer (known from weather)
year	1863	1861–65, Civil War (known from ''Rebel scouts'')
place	Gettysburg	Gettysburg (suggested by ''western Pennsylvania'')

Before you read the story that follows, look at Activity 3. Think about the questions as you read the story. Record your beginning and your ending times.

Freedom is an important part of American life. But not all people in America were always free. It took many years for some people to gain their freedom. In the story you are about to read, you will learn how one man fought for his freedom—and won.

Something to Lose _____

Written for this book
by Corinna Harmon.

When Joe was about seventeen, his owner James Betts smashed him on the side of the head with a stick. It has been a bad day with only a small crop harvested. When Betts told Joe to burn brush, Joe said he wouldn't on such a dry, windy day. Then the stick hit him.

James Betts stared at his slave. He felt horror and disgust over what he had done; he wished he could run away, hide, punish himself. His mind was boiling as he raised his arm to strike Joe again.

Joe knocked Betts to the ground, twisting the stick from the man's hand and holding it against his throat. He felt relaxed and balanced, his own blood cooling his cheek.

"I can kill you now," he said to Betts, who lay stunned beneath him. "If you ever hit me again, kill me, because I will surely kill you. I'm not afraid to die, so you can't frighten me. I can kill you now, but I'm letting you live."

Joe left the stick on Betts' throat and walked to his cabin to rinse his face. Supported by other slaves who had watched the fight, Betts stumbled to his house and lay on his bed beside the open window.

Betts was puzzled by his own feelings. Instead of anger or revenge, he felt relief. Always after he flogged a slave he felt dirty, guilty, and ashamed. But he did not

boulder (bōl′dēr), a very large rock.

murky (mūr′kē), dark or gloomy.

feel bad now, because Joe had beaten the fury out of him. Joe had already punished him; he did not have to punish himself.

In the white light outside he saw Joe walking away across the pasture carrying an iron rod as if it were a reed. Betts' constant feeling of loneliness fell away from him for a moment. He wasn't close to anyone—not his family, not his wife—but he felt close to Joe. Watching Joe's brown back, Betts fell asleep.

He never threatened Joe again.

While the slaves tore down a rotten rain gutter, they told stories they'd heard about the war between the colonists and the British. Silas swore that a slave who joined the army would earn his liberty at the end of the war.

Joe hoped to have Sadie for his wife, but he knew that their babies would be slaves and their grandchildren would be slaves. When Betts died, the black families might be split up and sold here and there. He'd rather be a soldier. At least he would become a free man, even though he would probably never see Sadie again.

He told Betts he needed a pass stating that he was not a runaway slave, so that he could join the army. Betts stuttered in confusion.

"I've enlisted myself. I'd had some comfort in thinking you'd be here on the farm, but I won't try to force you to stay."

And so it happened that master and slave served together in the war for American independence.

Lying on the ground Betts waited to fall asleep so he would lose consciousness of the cold. He dared not move after warming up a tiny patch of earth with his body heat. Spoiled food, blistered feet, heat, cold, thirst—nothing seemed to bother Joe. He didn't care. Nothing was bad or good; it just was. That was life.

During a battle, Betts often saw Joe through smoke and dust, standing easy, unaware of danger. He never seemed to duck, squint, dive, or cringe, even when a cannon ball snapped his shirt as it passed by. He dug trenches or loaded the cannon while men fell around him, as calm as if he were cutting hay. At first Betts thought Joe was the bravest man in the army, but then he remembered what Joe had said. Joe wasn't afraid to die.

One foggy night, Joe ran crouching along a stream to find out how far from his camp the British were camped. Within a mile he found them in a small valley. As he turned back to his camp, he stumbled in the stream, and a British guard shouted an alarm. Guns fired and a dozen men sprinted after him, pausing for a moment when they ran from the firelight into the dark. That was enough to give Joe a safe lead. Soon he saw the glow of his camp's fire ahead.

Leaping lightly onto a stone wall, he felt a small rock dislodge under his foot. As he fell sprawling on the ground, a boulder rolled onto his ankle, pinning him to the ground.

His pursuers reached the wall, some of

them stopping, some crossing it only yards from where Joe lay. He saw them against the murky sky, but they didn't see him in the meadow grass. He forced his breathing to slow down as they hunted him noisily. A boot stepped inches from his hand, laying the grass across his skin like a fan.

He heard a surprised yell from the Yankee camp, followed by a cry to follow the Redcoats! A clamor burst from the camp, and his pursuers turned tail. Laughing and grumbling, the Yankees stomped about where the British had stood.

"Get this boulder off my foot," said a quiet voice from the ground.

The ankle was not broken, but sprained and swollen. Joe sat under a tree for a few days. Betts saw that sometimes Joe shook his head and laughed to himself. Betts carried a bowl of stew to Joe and asked him what amused him.

"After I got back to camp the other night," Joe said, "I felt that everything inside me was wrong side up. I thought I had a fever or had eaten something bad. I figured out what it was—I was scared! When those Redcoats caught up to me I was afraid they were going to kill me. I had never felt scared before in my life, so I didn't know what it was."

"You were afraid of dying!" said Betts, laughing. "I guess that means you want to stay alive."

Joe's expression was both sour and amused.

"Why didn't you tell me that wanting to live felt the same as being sick?" he said.

After two years in the army Betts was wounded and returned to his farm. Joe served until the end of the war, when he received his freedom. Betts hired him as his farm manager, and in a few years Joe had earned enough to purchase Sadie out of slavery.

1 ACTIVITY

Fact Questions

Look in the story for the answers to the following questions. Write the answers on your paper.

1. How did James Betts feel when he struck his slave?

2. Why wasn't Joe afraid to fight his master?

3. How did Betts feel after Joe threatened him?

4. What reward did the slaves expect for fighting in the Revolution?

5. Why didn't Joe want to marry and stay on the farm?

6. What was unusual about Joe's attitude toward the hardships and dangers of war?

7. What kind of mission was Joe on when he was almost captured?

8. How did Joe describe the feeling of wanting to live?

9. What kind of work did Joe do after the war?

10. What did Joe do for Sadie?

Copy the chart on page 85 on your paper. Compute and record your WPM as you did on page 28.

Give yourself a score of 10 for each correct answer in Activity 1. This is your comprehension score. Record it on the chart.

	Hr.	Min.	Sec.
Ending time:	﹘﹘	﹘﹘	﹘﹘
Beginning time:	﹘﹘	﹘﹘	﹘﹘
Total Time:	﹘﹘	﹘﹘	﹘﹘

No. words: $\left(\dfrac{1084}{}\right) \times 60 =$ ﹘﹘﹘ **WPM**
No. seconds:

Comprehension Score: ﹘﹘﹘

ACTIVITY 3 — Thinking About Setting

1. Does the author describe the setting of this story directly, or does she suggest it indirectly?

2. Answer each question, and tell the words in the story that help you know each of the following:
   a. In what season does the story begin?
   b. In what historical period does the story take place?
   c. What was there about the setting that made it easier for Joe to hide from the British?

ACTIVITY 2 — Thought Questions

Think over the following questions carefully. Then write the answers on a separate sheet of paper.

1. If James Betts had wanted to prove that no slave could get away with hitting him, what would he have had to do to Joe?

2. How might another slaveholder judge Betts? Was he aware of his danger?

3. What do you think Joe would have done if Betts had refused him a pass to join the army?

4. How did Joe learn that he wanted to stay alive?

5. What was Joe willing to pay for his freedom?

85

**HOW TO READ IN
SOCIAL STUDIES**

In social studies reading, statements of fact and statements of opinion are often found in the same article, or even in the same paragraph. Confusing these two types of statements can cause serious problems.

A *fact* is a statement that can be proved true.

Example: Abraham Lincoln was the sixteenth president of the United States.

If you treat this fact as an opinion, you may waste time wondering whether it is correct, or even arguing with someone about whether Lincoln was the sixteenth or the seventeenth president. The only sensible way to settle this sort of factual question is simply to look it up in a reference book!

An *opinion* is a judgment or belief that seems right to an individual, but cannot be proved true or false.

Example A: Abraham Lincoln was our greatest president.
Example B: If Lincoln had not been president, there would have been no Civil War.

If you treat an opinion as a fact, you might make the mistake of accepting it as true without thinking very much about it. The most important things to remember about opinions are (1) different people have different opinions; (2) opinions may be changed; (3) careful thinkers have good reasons for their opinions.

How do you know when a statement in print is a fact? Very often dates and figures are given in a paragraph or article that is based on fact. Sometimes statements are made about things that scientists have found out by experimenting or observing. These statements may be accepted as facts. You are also safe in accepting as facts statements that are based on historical records.

Sometimes you may find phrases such as, "it is reported," "it is believed," or, "it is said." In these cases you should hold your decision in regard to the facts given until you get more evidence.

How can you tell when a statement is someone's opinion? Sometimes you will find phrases such as, "I think," "I believe," or, "it is my opinion." When you find this type of phrase, you know the writer is about to give an opinion. Other words that signal opinions are words that are used to make evaluations. *Good, better, beautiful, ugly, nice, bad,* and *worse* are examples of evaluating words.

Sometimes you will not find clues to tell you whether a statement is a fact or an opinion. Then you will just have to ask yourself, "Can this statement be proved, or not?"

While soldiers were fighting for independence in the battlefields, other patriots were fighting another kind of battle. In Philadelphia, a group of men were fighting a battle of words with the British government to try to preserve their rights. In the following article you will learn something about what happened during those battles.

Our Continental Congresses —

Written for this book
by Samuel Steinberg.

Although in 1774 the American colonists did not like British rule, few of them were ready to break with King George III. The delegates to the First Continental Congress met in Philadelphia in September of that year. Here they agreed to do nothing more than ask the British Government to repeal the hated Intolerable Acts. They felt that these acts were unfair. This appeal to the King contained no hint of any wish for independence. However, before the Congress finished its business, the members agreed to meet again in 1775, unless by then the British Government had given in. Thus, the First Continental Congress prepared the way for the second one.

King George turned down the colonists' appeal and gave orders to put an end to the "rebellion" by force. To carry out this order, the British Government blockaded all colonial ports and sent troops to seize the arms that the colonists had stored

in Concord, near Boston. The "Minutemen," alerted by Paul Revere's ride, ambushed the British soldiers, killing many of them. Thus the King's order had turned an imaginary rebellion into a real one.

The Second Continental Congress, which met in Philadelphia on May 10, 1775, was made up of delegates from every American colony. Like the First Continental Congress, it sent appeals to the British Government. It asked Great Britain to repeal the laws that affected our Colonial trade and to withdraw the hated troops. The British Government refused this appeal.

So the Second Continental Congress stayed in session and adopted three strong measures against the mother country. These measures were (1) declaring independence from Great Britain; (2) adopting military measures (which, of course, meant war); and (3) forming a national government. These great tasks were to be carried out by committees and boards in the Congress.

How was it possible for a single body of men to do such things at a time when each colony considered itself independent from the others? One reason was that leaders in the Congress agreed with Benjamin Franklin's belief that they must "all

---

repeal (ri pēl′), do away with.

Intolerable Acts (in tol′ər ə bl akts), certain British trade laws which the colonists felt were unbearable.

rebellion (ri bel′yən), refusal to obey the government.

blockade (blok ād′), prevent ships from leaving or entering a port.

ambush (am′bush), attack from a hidden position.

Washington taking command of the Army

Delegates to the First Continental Congress

hang together in order not to hang separately." Another reason was that the Second Continental Congress was made up of the wisest and most powerful men who lived in America at that time. Some of these men became governors of the states. Some became judges. There were even three future presidents of the United States among them. Wise men with a deep desire for unity account for the success of the Second Continental Congress.

One of the first acts of the Congress was to elect George Washington Commander-in-Chief of the Continental Army. Members of the Congress thought that he was the best man not only to lead the army, but also to inspire the people to fight for freedom. Only about a third of the population was in favor of the Revolution when Washington took command. The rest either did not care or were really opposed to it. As one historian said, "Washington was the soul of the American cause."

One of the greatest acts the world has ever known was the adoption of the Declaration of Independence by the Second Continental Congress on July 4, 1776. Thomas Jefferson showed great wisdom in writing this declaration. He felt that it was not enough to hate and fight the enemy. He believed that it was also important for the people to prove their love for democracy. In reading the first two paragraphs of the Declaration, we can see how well Jefferson expressed this love for democracy. The Declaration of Independence won support at home; it also won friends abroad. It set up ideals for future generations, not only in America, but wherever people fought for the freedom to govern themselves.

ACTIVITY 1 — Fact or Opinion

The following six sentences are taken from the article you just read. Read each one. Decide whether it expresses a fact or an opinion. Write the numbers 1 through 6 on a separate paper. Next to each number, write *Fact* if the sentence with that number expresses a fact, or *Opinion* if the sentence with that number expresses an opinion.

1. The Second Continental Congress, which met in Philadelphia on May 10, 1775, was made up of delegates from every American colony.

2. Some of these men became governors of the states.

3. Wise men with a deep desire for unity account for the success of the Second Continental Congress.

4. One of the first acts of the Congress was to elect George Washington Commander-in-Chief of the Continental Army.

5. One of the greatest acts the world has ever known was the adoption of the Declaration of Independence by the Second Continental Congress on July 4, 1776.

6. Thomas Jefferson showed great wisdom in writing this declaration.

ACTIVITY 2 — On Your Own

On your paper, write two fact sentences and two opinion sentences of your own. Label your sentences *Fact* or *Opinion*.

Franklin introduced to the King of France

HOW TO READ IN SCIENCE

Geologists study rocks to find out what happened to the earth millions of years ago—how mountains were formed, where seas once covered the land, and even what plants and animals lived in different periods of the earth's history. When you read geology articles like the one that follows, look for two main types of information—cause and effect, and classification. Geologists explain causes and effects when they tell how different rocks and land structures were formed. They classify types of rocks and land formations into groups according to their similarities and differences.

1. First *scan* the article to find the cause-and-effect paragraphs. Some clue words and phrases that will help you to identify cause-and-effect paragraphs are *the results, because, caused, the cause of,* and *the reason is.* Don't read the selection carefully at this time; simply *scan* for the above phrases in order to locate the cause-and-effect paragraphs.

2. *Scan* again for paragraphs that have to do with classifications. Clue phrases to look for are *three different kinds* and *three different stages.*

3. Now you are ready to read the selection carefully. Read the cause-and-effect paragraphs, looking especially for explanations of how and why things have happened. Read the classification paragraphs for the purpose of finding out what the classifications are and what makes each one different.

4. Record your beginning and ending times.

Fossil of shark imbedded in shale

The original thirteen Colonies that became the United States of America extended only along a small portion of the Atlantic coast. Now the land our ancestors fought for stretches between two oceans and includes some of the world's greatest natural wonders. One of these is the Grand Canyon in Arizona.

How Geologists Read the History of the Earth

Written for this book
by Gordon E. Van Hooft.

The beautiful scenery of the Grand Canyon in Arizona and the scenery of similar canyons are of chief interest to tourists. To the scientists who study rocks, however, the sides of these canyons reveal many facts about the earth's history. How do these geologists read the history of the earth in layers of rocks, and what story is told?

The Grand Canyon is one of our deepest canyons. The sightseer standing on the rim of the Grand Canyon sees the results of a million years' work of wind and moving water. Once the Colorado River flowed over fairly level ground. Now it is flowing at the bottom of a canyon about one mile deep, more than eight miles wide, and 300 miles long. Over the years the river and its branches have slowly worn down and carried away tons of rock. We can see in the steep canyon walls several layers of rocks.

As we go deeper and deeper into the canyon, we see all about us rocks that were

sedimentary (sed'ə men'tə rē), referring to the matter that settles at the bottom of a liquid.

fossil (fos'l), the hardened remains or trace of an animal or plant left in rock.

Archean (är'kē ən), referring to the oldest known group of rocks in the earth's crust.

formed earlier and earlier in the past. The lowest layers are the oldest, because they were formed first. The canyon walls give us a general outline of much of the earth's history, chapter by chapter.

While the upper or more recent layers are horizontal, many of the lower or older layers are tipped or tilted. Geologists are interested in the cause of these uneven layers. They know that great forces have been at work either lifting one end and lowering the other or pressing sideways to cause the rock layers to fold. You can readily understand this process of folding if you push toward the middle from the ends of a stack of thin sheets of colored modeling clay. Then cut down through the hump or "mountain" to see the curved layers. Perhaps you have noticed tilted or folded rock layers where a road or railroad has been cut through some natural mound of rock.

Sometimes one can see cracks in rock layers. These are caused by rocks which have broken and have slid apart. The rock layers are no longer continuous, but suddenly end at a crack, which is called a *fault*. The layers are either higher or lower on the other side of the fault.

The pressure of the ocean is very great. It squeezes particles of soil, sand, shells, and dead sea animals solidly together. The result is a hard substance known as *sedimentary rock*. In places where there was once a sea or a large body of water, you can still find layers of rock which were made in this manner.

There are three kinds of sedimentary rock. One kind is limestone, which is composed chiefly of animal shells and coral. Another kind is sandstone. This rock is made up of grains of sand. The beautiful red and yellow bands seen on the walls of the Grand Canyon are layers of different kinds of sand which were pressed into rock

by an ocean. A third kind of sedimentary rock is called shale. This rock is made by water pressure on mud that contains the remains of plant and animal life.

Fossils are found in sedimentary rocks. Fossils are the remains or forms of plants and animals preserved in the rock. In the Grand Canyon, fossils have been found in all layers of rocks except one. There are no fossils in the black Archean rock at the bottom of the canyon, because at the time the Archean layer was formed, no visible forms of life existed on earth.

Fossils reveal three different stages in the development of life. In the first stage there were only plant forms. These plant forms were very simple and grew in water only. The second stage was the sea-animal, bird-and-insect, land-plant stage. During this stage, simple sea animals, fish, and reptiles appeared in the ocean. Birds and insects began to live on the land, and plants began to grow on land. Then came the third stage of complex plants and mammals. These complex plants and mammals are ancestors of the plants and animals that we know today. This slow development of living things from simple to complex forms is a story written in the rocks for all to read.

Copy this chart on your paper. Compute and record your WPM as you did on page 28.

	Hr.	Min.	Sec.
Ending time:	_____	_____	_____
Beginning time:	_____	_____	_____
Total Time:	_____	_____	_____
No. words: No. seconds:	$\left(\dfrac{713}{\quad}\right) \times 60 =$		_____ **WPM**

ACTIVITY **Stating Causes**

On your paper, write the cause of each effect listed below.

1. The Grand Canyon is one of our deepest canyons.

2. Many of the older layers are tipped or tilted.

3. Sometimes one can see cracks in layers.

4. The result is a hard substance known as sedimentary rock.

5. There are no fossils in the black Archean rock at the bottom of the canyon.

ACTIVITY **Classifying**

On a separate sheet of paper, name three kinds of sedimentary rock. Opposite each name tell what makes that rock different from the other kinds.

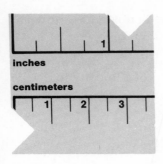

inches

centimeters

1   2   3

In this lesson you will be working with the metric system. You will have to *read* tables, and use the tables in doing the activities. This means that you will look back and forth between the tables and sentences in the activities. The ability to do this is important for reading in social studies and science as well as mathematics.

As you read the following article, concentrate on practicing this reading skill.

HOW TO READ IN MATHEMATICS

The American Revolution was not the only revolution of its time. In 1789 the French people revolted against their government. After the French Revolution, in 1799, the new French government created a new system of measures known as the *metric system.*

The Metric System _____

Written for this book
by William L. Schaaf.

The metric system of measures uses the *meter* as its standard of length. The meter was first defined as being exactly one ten-millionth part of the distance on the earth's surface from the North Pole to the equator. But for practical purposes it was never possible to obtain an exact figure for this measurement. So in 1889 the meter was defined in another way, and was called the International Prototype Meter. In 1960 a new international definition of the meter was adopted, based on an unchanging natural standard: the wavelength of the light given off by electrified krypton in a vacuum. In all cases, the meter is roughly equal to 39.37 inches.

krypton (krip′tän), a colorless gas present in small amounts in the atmosphere, used in high-powered light bulbs.

Today the metric system is either official or is legally allowed in every country in the world.

The meter is divided into smaller units, as shown in this table.

$$0.1 \text{ meter} = 1 \text{ decimeter}$$
$$0.01 \text{ meter} = 1 \text{ centimeter}$$
$$0.001 \text{ meter} = 1 \text{ millimeter}$$

Notice that *deci* means $\frac{1}{10}$, or 0.1; *centi* means $\frac{1}{100}$, or 0.01; and *milli* means $\frac{1}{1000}$, or 0.001.

We can also say the following:

$$10 \text{ decimeters} = 1 \text{ meter}$$
$$100 \text{ centimeters} = 1 \text{ meter}$$
$$1000 \text{ millimeters} = 1 \text{ meter}$$

ACTIVITY 1

Answer these questions on a separate piece of paper.

1. **a.** How many centimeters are there in a meter?

   b. One meter is how many times as long as a centimeter?

2. **a.** How many millimeters are there in a meter?

   b. One meter is how many times as long as a millimeter?

3. **a.** How many millimeters are there in a centimeter?

   b. A centimeter is how many times as long as a millimeter?

ACTIVITY 2

Another unit of length is the *yard*, which is defined by law as follows:

1 U.S. yard = 0.9144 meter, *exactly.*

This legal definition makes an inch *exactly* equal to 2.54 cm., and makes the meter *approximately* 39.37 inches long.

Copy the following chart onto your paper. Use the two rulers to fill in the missing measurements on the chart. Answer to the closest $\frac{1}{4}$ inch or $\frac{1}{2}$ centimeter. The first one has been filled in for you.

	Inches	Centimeters
1.	3	$7\frac{1}{2}$
2.		10
3.	$5\frac{1}{2}$	
4.		4
5.	$3\frac{1}{2}$	
6.		12

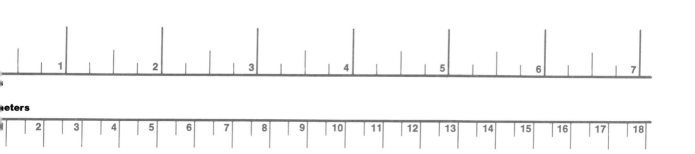

95

Finding Major and Minor Details in Paragraphs

Minor details grow out of major details. They are not as important as major details, but in studying some subjects it is important that you grasp the minor details as well as the major details. The paragraphs in the next article have both major and minor details. See how well you can show how minor details grow out of major details.

1. A block diagram has been made of the first paragraph. Study this as a sample. Notice that only important words and phrases have been written for all sentences except the main idea sentence.

2. When you have finished studying paragraph 1, get a sheet of paper. Make block diagrams for all the remaining paragraphs in the article. In some cases you may wish to write an entire sentence to give the meaning. In most cases you may pick out only the important words and phrases in the sentences.

Peter Salem[2]

1. Peter Salem was a slave who wanted to fight in the Revolutionary War. His master, Major Lawson Buckminster, was very patriotic. He was angered because the British were charging the Colonies taxes on goods without their consent.

Peter heard his master speak about a possible war. He had said that guns and ammunition had been hidden by farmers and tradesmen. He also had said that hundreds, even thousands, of men would be needed.

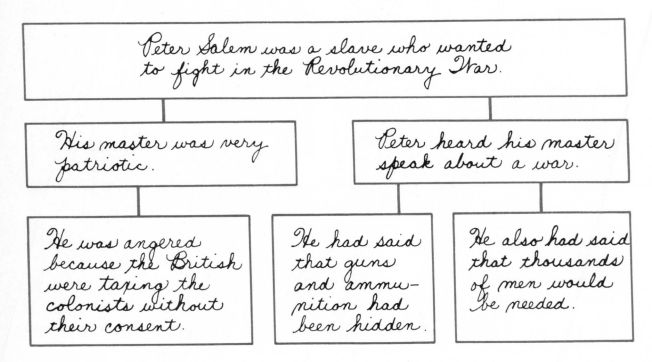

Peter Salem was a slave who wanted to fight in the Revolutionary War.

His master was very patriotic.

Peter heard his master speak about a war.

He was angered because the British were taxing the colonists without their consent.

He had said that guns and ammunition had been hidden.

He also had said that thousands of men would be needed.

Buckminster (buk min′stər), the last name of the man who owned Peter Salem as a slave.

Pitcairn (pit′kārn), the last name of a British major in the Revolutionary War.

2. Because Peter Salem was eager to fight the British, Major Buckminster gave him permission to join a company of Minutemen. The company was headed by Captain Simon Edgell. There were seventy-five men in his company. All of the men were from Framingham, Massachusetts.

3. Peter served in this company for five days, April 19 through April 23. He joined the company just in time to fight in the first battles of the Revolution. On April 19 he fought at Lexington. On the same day he fought at Concord.

4. After serving with the Minutemen at Concord, Peter joined a company in the 5th Massachusetts Regiment. The regiment was led by Colonel John Nixon. The colonel and the men in his regiment had very little training. However, Colonel Nixon rushed his men forward to help fight at Breed's Hill and Bunker Hill.

5. The leader of the British forces at Bunker Hill was John Pitcairn, a famous British major. During the battle, Major Pitcairn rushed into the midst of the fighting. He wanted to urge his men on to defeat the colonists. He rode right up to the high mound of earth that the colonists had thrown up. He got no farther, for he was shot. Many historians believe that Peter Salem fired the shot that killed Major Pitcairn.

6. Today a memorial tombstone honors Peter Salem. The memorial reads in part: "Peter Salem, a soldier of the Revolution." On patriotic holidays, a flag flies over Peter Salem's grave. It is the flag of the country that Peter helped to make possible.

Outlining Paragraphs

You have made block diagrams of paragraphs with major and minor details. Sometimes when you are studying detailed material you may wish to outline paragraphs as a means of helping you to grasp the information.

Read the following article. Study the outline for paragraph 1, which has been made for you. Make your own outlines for the other paragraphs. Be sure to use Roman numerals (I, II, III) for the main ideas, capital letters (A, B, C) for the major details, and Arabic numerals (1, 2, 3) for the minor details. In some cases you may have to write an entire sentence. In some cases you will need to write only the important words and phrases. (You should begin your outline of paragraph 2 with Roman numeral II.)

The Articles of Confederation and the Constitution

1. In 1781, the Second Continental Congress adopted the Articles of Confederation, an agreement by which the original thirteen Colonies established a central government. The Articles of Confederation gave the central government certain powers. Congress was granted the power to declare war and peace, establish an army and navy, manage foreign affairs, issue and borrow money, and control Indian affairs. But the Articles reflected the strong distrust the colonists had for a powerful central government. It guaranteed each state independence, gave each state all powers not specifically granted to Congress, and did not allow Congress to collect taxes or control trade.

2. George Washington, Alexander Hamilton, and other members of Congress felt that, under the Articles of Confederation, the federal government was too weak to hold the new nation together. In 1787, the Continental Congress met in Philadelphia to revise and improve the Articles. Instead, the convention drafted a new constitution which set up the federal system of government we have today.

3. The Constitution divided powers between the national government, the state governments, and individual citizens. It gave Congress more powers than the Articles of Confederation. Among these were the power to collect taxes and the power to regulate trade. It also granted Congress implied powers — the power to take actions which may not be specifically mentioned in the Constitution, but which may be made necessary by changing conditions in the future. The Constitution reserved certain rights for the states. Among these were the rights to legislate on divorce, marriage, and public education. The Bill of Rights is the part of the Constitution that protects the rights of each individual citizen from various unjust acts of government.

Paragraph 1

1. In 1781, the Second Continental Congress adopted the Articles of Confederation, an agreement by which the Colonies established a central government.
   A. The Articles of Confederation gave the government certain powers.
      1. declare war and peace
      2. establish an army and navy
      3. manage foreign affairs
      4. issue and borrow money
      5. control Indian affairs

B. The Articles reflected the distrust the colonists had for a powerful central government.

    1. It guaranteed each state independence.

    2. It gave each state all powers not specifically granted to Congress.

    3. It did not allow Congress to collect taxes or control trade.

Dividing Words Into Syllables

In Unit 3, you had practice in some of the ways of dividing words into syllables. Now you will have practice in two more ways of deciding at what point to break a word into syllables.

A. Guide 5: Considering Consonant Blends as Single Consonants. You have learned that a consonant blend consists of two or three consonants that are blended together to make just one sound. *Tr, str, cl,* and *pl* are examples of consonant blends. Since a consonant blend is just one sound, you usually consider the blend as a single consonant when you divide a word. Sometimes the word will then be divided according to Guide 3, between separately sounded consonants. For instance, the word *instruct* is divided *in struct* because *str* is considered as one consonant. Other words with consonant blends may be divided according to Guide 4: When a word contains a single consonant between two sounded vowels, divide (a) *after* the consonant if the first vowel is short, and (b) *before* the consonant if the first vowel is long or has a sound that is neither long nor short. For example, the word *migrate* is divided *mi grate* because the first vowel is long. On your paper, divide these words according to the guide.

1. fragrant
2. reclaim
3. complete
4. extreme
5. conclude
6. express
7. recline
8. hamster

Note these exceptions to Guide 5: When a word ends in *ble, cle, dle, gle, ple, tle,* and similar formations, these letters make a syllable by themselves, as in *cra dle.*
Divide these words on your paper:

9. bundle
10. trouble
11. people
12. mangle

B. Guide 6: Dividing Between Prefixes and Base Words. Prefixes, base words, and suffixes are syllables or combinations of syllables in themselves. When dividing a word made up of these elements, you often divide between them.
Here are some words with prefixes. On your paper, divide them according to the guide.

1. unless
2. exchange
3. inquire
4. reread
5. enlarge
6. preview
7. unfair
8. recall
9. submerge
10. import
11. context
12. surround

C. Guide 7: Dividing Between Base Words and Suffixes. Usually, we divide between the base word and the suffix. There are some exceptions to this guide, however. The base word often gives a final consonant, especially *t,* to a suffix. The word *active,* for instance, is divided *ac tive* because it would be difficult to pronounce *act ive.* Once you get a word broken into small enough parts so that you can test various ways of pronouncing it, you usually won't have any trouble finding the cases in which the final consonant of the base word has been added to the suffix to make pronunciation easier.
In the following list of words, there are words to which suffixes have been added. Two of the words are exceptions to the guide. On your paper, divide the words. Circle the two exceptions.

1. leaflet
2. statement
3. freedom
4. blockade
5. threaten
6. rooter
7. safely
8. helpful
9. actor
10. harmful
11. grayish
12. collection

Working with Social Studies Words

The words below are used frequently in social studies and history textbooks. If you know the pronunciation and meaning of these words, it will be helpful to you in your studying.

Work out the pronunciation of each word. Say the word distinctly. Study the meaning of the word and think about it.

---

amendment (ə mend′mənt), a change, correction, or addition made in the Constitution or a bill.

campaign (kam pān′), a series of military acts forming a distinct stage of a war; the efforts of a political party to get its candidates elected.

compromise (kom′prə mīz), a settlement in a dispute reached by agreement of the people concerned or their representatives.

Constitution (kon′stə tōō′shən), in American history this means the written statements of principles and rules of our government.

delegate (del′ə gāt), one sent by others and given the power to act for them.

disarmament (dis är′mə mənt), laying aside or taking away weapons; reduction of armies, navies, and their equipment.

Frigid Zone (fri′jid zōn), either of two polar regions of the earth; Arctic or Antarctic.

priority (prī ôr′ə te), degree of importance.

Temperate Zone (tem′pər it zōn), either of two parts of the earth between the tropics and polar regions; temperature never reaches extremes of hot or cold.

Torrid Zone (tôr′id zōn), the very warm region of the earth; the tropics.

See if you know the meaning of each of these words as used in social studies. On your paper, write the word that belongs in each blank space. You will need to add *s* to some of the words.

1. John Paul Jones waged a great _____ when he fought English ships during the Revolution.

2. The document which states our government's basic law and principles and supreme law of the land is called the _____.

3. At a meeting of Congress, a change can be made in the Constitution. Such a change to the Constitution is called an

   _____.

4. The United States government places a high _____ on the defense of our nation.

5. Henry Clay wanted to settle the slave question by an agreement between the North and the South. He believed in

   _____.

6. Indonesia has a very hot climate. It is located in the _____.

7. At the end of many wars, the winning side insists on _____ of the defeated troops.

8. Exploring Antarctica is difficult since it is in the _____.

9. All of the members of Congress cannot go to a meeting in a distant country. So they send one person to act as their

   _____.

10. The greatest number of people live where it is never extremely hot or cold. They live in the _____.

5

Other Worlds

**HOW TO READ
LITERATURE**

In the last story you read, you started thinking about setting. Knowing details about what a place looks like and feels like can help you enjoy a story. Sometimes, however, the setting is more than just something that adds to your enjoyment. Sometimes the setting is the most important part of a story.

In the science fiction story you will read next, the setting is so important that if it were different, the whole story would have to change. As you read the story, think about the details of the setting that make the story happen the way it does. Why does the story have to take place where it does?

Record your beginning and ending time.

103

How would you like to live on another planet? Or maybe you'd rather just visit one. In the next story, you will learn more about what such an experience might be like.

A Bridge Through Space _____

Written for this book
by Juliana O. Muehrcke.

"The spaceship's landing!" Dad called. "Come on!"

"Do I *have* to?" I grumbled. "It's just a lot of tourists from Earth."

"One of the scientists from Earth is bringing his son Danny along," Dad said. "He's sixteen, just your age. I want you to make him feel at home."

"I get so tired of people coming from Earth to study Mars," I said. "They use up our air and water and food, and all they do is gawk at us."

But, for Dad's sake, I decided I'd try to be friendly. I went to meet the spaceship.

I was born on Mars. My parents were on one of the first spaceships from Earth to Mars, at the beginning of the twenty-first century.

Things have changed a lot since then. Two thousand people live here now, under a huge plastic dome. The artificial air in the dome is kept at the same temperature all the time. Without the dome, of course, we'd be at the mercy of the quickly changing Martian weather.

Whenever we leave the dome, we have to wear breathing suits. The air on Mars is too thin and low in oxygen for us to breathe.

I watched the passengers climbing off the spaceship. There was Danny now. He had reached the ground and was taking big bouncy steps. His boots threw up puffs of yellow sand. "It feels so funny!" he cried. "It's like flying!"

I went toward him. "That's because the gravity is only one-third what it is on Earth," I told Danny. "But try not to jump around so much. It uses up air for no good reason. Air is precious on Mars."

Danny stopped bouncing, but he didn't answer. He just stared at me wide-eyed. How rude these earthlings were!

To hide my anger, I started hauling crates from the ship. Danny's eyes grew even rounder. I chuckled to myself, guessing his thoughts. I must seem incredibly strong, carrying such big boxes so easily. He didn't realize that the light gravity on Mars made physical work a lot easier than it would be on Earth.

Boy, did he have a lot to learn!

He was still gaping at me—as if I were a freak. "What did you expect?" I wanted to say. "Little green men?"

Friendship with this earthling was impossible, no matter what Dad said. I turned my back on Danny and walked off across the sand. All around me the desert stretched as far as the eye could see, flat and barren.

On Earth, I had learned, there were mountains and jungles and great oceans. It was hard to imagine.

There were no oceans here or lakes or rivers. No water at all. No rain, or even clouds. We have to make our own water here. We make it chemically, just as we make our air. We make most of our own food, too. Life on Mars is completely artificial. It's the only way human life can survive here.

What did a mountain look like? I wondered. And a cloud? How would it be to breathe real Earth air? To climb mountain peaks and walk in tall green forests?

There were no trees here — only a few twisted, stumpy plants. No mountains — just an endless stretch of loose yellow sand or dry red dust.

I knew there were deserts on Earth, too. Parts of Arizona, I had read, looked something like Mars. But I still had this childish picture of Earth being all green and blue — as brightly colored as our Martian rocks.

I had hoped to ask Danny about Earth. Now of course I couldn't. He thought of me only as some weird creature to study. Anger rose again as I remembered his rude stare.

Later, I went back to the dome and sat watching the stars come out — billions of them like bright dust in the black sky. A blue-green dot glowed large and clear among them. *That*, I knew, was Earth, forty million miles away.

Danny came in, shivering. "Boy, it's chilly out there!"

I grunted. "Turn up your space heater if you're cold."

"Mars is fascinating, isn't it?" Danny said. "I'd love to have you show me around.

"I'm not a tour guide," I snapped.

Danny didn't take the hint. "It's a lot warmer on Mars than I expected," he said.

"It was nearly seventy degrees this afternoon. How cold does it get at night?"

"Around zero," I said. "Of course we're on the equator here. At the poles it gets a lot colder." When would he get tired of studying me like some creature under a microscope?

"Wow! How can you live where it's so warm in the daytime and so cold at night?"

I was getting really annoyed. To think Dad wanted me to be *friends* with this earthling! All Danny wanted to do was quiz me. As if he were writing a geography paper about me!

Despite his lack of manners, I tried to answer politely. "We stay under the dome most of the time. Whenever we leave the dome, we adjust the heat controls on the suits we wear."

"Still," Danny said, "you must be awfully hardy to put up with such rapid temperature changes."

That was the last straw. "I'm no different from you!" I shouted. "I may be a Martian, but I'm still a human being!"

"So am I!" Danny said, angry now too. "I've tried to be friendly, but I'm sick of your treating me like a—a creature from another planet."

"That's what you are, aren't you?" I snapped back.

I stormed out, seething with anger. Well, at least I'd gotten the last word.

All at once I felt sick and dizzy. Oh, my gosh! I'd forgotten my breathing suit!

I staggered back toward the dome. Then everything went black.

When I opened my eyes, Danny was bending over me, holding an oxygen mask to my mouth.

"Are you all right?" he asked. "Gee, I'm sorry I upset you, asking all those questions. It's just that I'm so excited to be here. All my life I've wanted to come to Mars."

I sucked in air. Why, Danny wasn't being rude, I realized. He was merely as curious about my planet as I was about his.

"Isn't it strange," I said, "that people can travel from one planet to another, but two people can't communicate any better than they could a century ago? It's too bad, isn't it?"

"Yes," Danny said. "Especially when we have so much to teach each other."

"You saved my life," I said. "That was quick thinking."

"What are friends for?" Danny said.

I smiled. "And I thought I was so smart. What a dumb thing for me to do!"

Danny smiled back. "We all make mistakes," he said. "After all, we're only human."

ACTIVITY 1

Fact Questions

1. Why do people on Mars wear breathing suits?

2. Why is physical work easier on Mars than on Earth?

3. How does the narrator feel Danny is looking at her?

4. How much natural water is there on Mars?

5. Where do people on Mars get their water?

6. Where do people on Mars get their food?

7. Name a few things Earth has that Mars doesn't.

8. What does Earth look like from Mars?

9. How far from Mars is Earth?

10. Why did Danny ask so many questions?

Copy this chart on your paper. Compute and record your WPM as you did on page 28.

Give yourself a score of 10 for each correct answer in Activity 1. This is your comprehension score. Record it on the chart.

	Hr.	Min.	Sec.
Ending time:	_____	_____	_____
Beginning time:	_____	_____	_____
Total Time:	_____	_____	_____

No. words: $\left(\dfrac{1153}{\text{No. seconds}}\right) \times 60 =$ _____ **WPM**

Comprehension score: _____

ACTIVITY 2 — Thought Questions

1. What was the narrator's attitude toward Danny, even before the two met?

2. What experiences caused the narrator to dislike Danny even before she met him?

3. Put yourself in the narrator's place. Would you consider Danny's questions rude? Why, or why not?

ACTIVITY 3 — Thinking About Setting

1. Where does the story take place?

2. When does the story take place?

3. In a few words, describe each of the following:
   a. the surface of Mars
   b. the plants on Mars
   c. the weather on Mars

4. How would the story change if the setting were different?

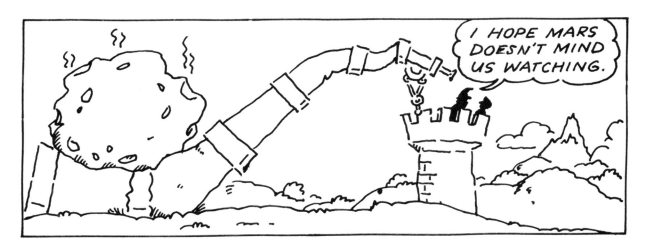

I HOPE MARS DOESN'T MIND US WATCHING.

HOW TO READ IN SOCIAL STUDIES

Some of the most interesting articles you will read in social studies will be about an author's theory on some particular subject. A theory is an explanation that has not been proved. Often, a theory is formulated to solve a "mystery." For example, certain diseases are not caused by bacteria. Doctors knew this, but they could not find the causes for these diseases. They formed a theory that diseases not caused by bacteria are caused by other organisms they called *viruses*. But no one had ever seen a virus. Now that viruses have been seen under the electron microscope, the theory has been proved. It can now be considered a fact that viruses exist.

Another example is the theory that explains why dinosaurs became extinct. Fossils of these huge animals had been found, but no such animals were known to exist in the history of the human race. Scientists reasoned that they once existed, but for some reason died out. The question was, "Why?" Scientists also knew that the earth had undergone drastic changes at different periods of its history. They formed a theory that dinosaurs became extinct because they could not adapt to rapid changes in the earth's climate and vegetation. This theory will never be proved, because we cannot go back in time. However, the theory is believable, since it takes all the facts into consideration, and there are no known facts to contradict it.

In reading social studies material, you should question the author's theories. Think about the facts the author gives, and facts you already know on the subject. You may even want to look for more information. Then, decide whether you accept the theory. Ask yourself these questions:

1. Do the facts support the theory?
2. Does the theory explain *all* the facts, or are there still some "left-over" facts that don't fit in?
3. Are there any facts that contradict the theory?

When you read the following article, think of these questions. Use the map that accompanies the article to get the facts clear in your mind.

Anthropologists study different cultures in different parts of the world to find out more about the human race. From the facts they learn, they form theories to explain how groups of people have developed customs and traditions, and how they have adapted to their environments. The following article explains how anthropologists took a puzzling set of facts about the Eskimos and developed a theory that seems to solve the puzzle.

The Eskimos— Solving the Puzzle

The original inhabitants of northwestern Alaska are the Eskimos, a people with their own unique traditions and customs. Eskimos are found also in northeastern Russia, northern Canada, and

unique (ū nēk'), single; unlike any other.

Greenland. Although individual groups of Eskimos differ slightly from one another in their ways of life, their traditional clothing, houses, methods of hunting and preparing food, and their languages are closely similar. There is no other culture in the world which is like that of the Eskimos.

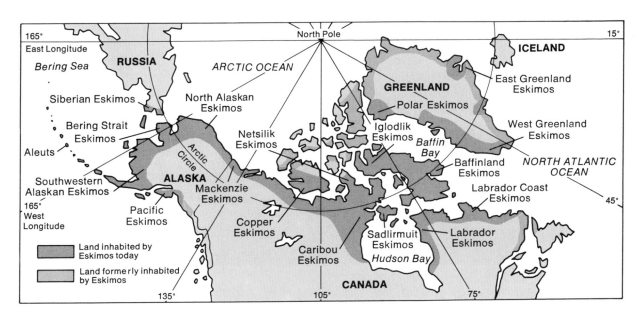

Anthropologists are interested in studying the Eskimos because of their unique culture and because they are scattered from Russia to northwestern Alaska and across North America. The existence in different places of people so similar to each other, yet so unlike any other culture seemed puzzling. Searching for an explanation, anthropologists formed a theory that where the Bering Strait is today, there was once a land bridge connecting Alaska with the part of Russia now called Siberia. (See map.) According to the theory, the first Eskimo lived on this land bridge more than 10,000 years ago. Some of them moved east to what is now Alaska, and later migrated further eastward across the Arctic to North America and Greenland. Others moved west to Siberia. This theory is widely accepted today.

ACTIVITY 1 — Listing the Facts

On a separate sheet of paper, list the facts in the article that are explained by the land-bridge theory. Number the facts. (You should find at least three.)

ACTIVITY 2 — Judging the Theory

1. On your paper, briefly explain the land-bridge theory.

2. Check the facts you listed for Activity 1. Decide whether or not you feel the theory satisfactorily explains the facts. Write on your paper, "The theory makes sense to me," or, "The theory does not make sense to me."

HOW TO READ IN SCIENCE

This selection is similar to some of the material you find in your science books. It gives information which scientists have found by observing the planets. It doesn't explain a process; it isn't a problem-solving or classification selection. It just gives straight information. Science selections of this type are easier to read and can be read more rapidly than other types. If you wish to get detailed facts about some particular part, then you need to go back and reread that part more carefully.

1. Read through the entire selection rapidly for general information. Time yourself. When you have finished, do Activity 1 to find out how much general information you have gained in this first rapid reading.

2. Suppose that during rapid reading, you became especially interested in details about one of the planets. Go back to the section on that planet. Find the main idea.

You have read a science fiction story about Mars, but there are other planets in the skies. The following selection is full of interesting facts about our neighbors in space.

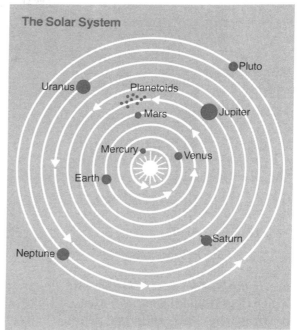

The Solar System

Our Neighbors in Space _____

Written for this book
by Irving Zeichner.

In addition to Earth, there are eight other planets traveling around the sun in huge orbits. The sun and this family of planets make up the solar system. The members of this family are our nearest neighbors in space.

The sun is a giant mass of burning gases over a million times larger than the Earth and is about 93 million miles (149 million kilometers) from the Earth.

Closest to the sun is the tiny planet

Mercury. This is the smallest and fastest of the planets, and it is only 36 million miles (58 million kilometers) from the sun. The side of Mercury which faces the center of the solar system is very hot—scientists believe over 700°F (371°C).

The planet next in order is Venus. Dense clouds cover the surface of Venus and reflect a great deal of sunlight. This is why Venus shines brighter in our evening sky than any other body in space except the moon. Telescopes cannot peer through the clouds, so we know little about the surface of Venus.

The planet next in order is Earth. Earth is the first planet to be circled by a little follower or satellite, the moon. The moon is a ball of rock about 2,000 miles (3,200

---

atmosphere (at′məs fêr), air surrounding the Earth.

orbit (ôr′bit), the path that is traveled by a planet.

solar system (sō′lər sis′təm), the sun and all the planets that revolve around it.

113

kilometers) in diameter and only about 240,000 miles (384,000 kilometers) away. The moon shines by light reflected from the sun. There is no air or water on the moon, making it impossible for life as we know it to exist there.

Mars is the next planet after ours in the solar system. Mars has two very small moons, one of which circles the planet about three times each day. The atmosphere of Mars has been of interest to scientists because they have thought that some kind of life might exist there. Careful examination with special instruments has shown that Mars has an atmosphere containing a small amount of oxygen and some water vapor. This planet goes through changes of season similar to those on Earth. A scientist's telescope reveals something that looks like ice caps in the regions that are having winter. As spring and summer come, the ice seems to melt. Then, large blue-green patches appear on the reddish surface of Mars. These patches of green have been thought to be some kind of simple plant life similar to algae and mosses. Although the Viking I probes in 1976 found no evidence of plant life, future probes may yet prove the theory. There has never been any evidence, however, of animal or human life on Mars.

Jupiter, the largest planet, is fifth in order from the sun. Nearly 90,000 miles (144,000 kilometers) in diameter, Jupiter takes about 12 earth-years to journey around the sun. Its atmosphere is made of poisonous gases which show as light and dark bands when seen through a telescope. Jupiter has 12 moons.

Saturn is next in order and is very cold because it is over 800 million miles (1,280 million kilometers) from the sun.

Uranus and Neptune are next in order. These planets are very large and are two and three billion miles (3.2 and 4.8 billion kilometers) from the sun. They cannot be seen without the help of a powerful telescope.

Pluto, the last planet in order, was discovered in 1930. It is a small planet about which little is known because of its great distance from Earth. Some scientists believe that Pluto was originally an escaped moon of Neptune.

ACTIVITY 1   **Checking Information**

Use your own paper.

1. The solar system is made up of the Earth, eight other planets, and what else?

2. Which is larger, the sun or the Earth?

3. Which is the smallest of the planets?

4. Which planet is covered with dense clouds?

5. What is the Earth's little follower?

6. Why would it be impossible for life to exist on the moon?

7. More information was given about one of the planets than the others. What was that planet?

8. Is there evidence of animal life on Mars?

9. Which planet is covered with poisonous gases?

10. What do some people think Pluto is?

Copy this chart on your paper. Compute and record your WPM as you did on page 28.

Give yourself a score of 10 for each correct answer in Activity 1. This is your comprehension score. Record it on the chart.

	Hr.	Min.	Sec.
Ending time:	____	____	____
Beginning time:	____	____	____
Total Time:	____	____	____

No. words:
No. seconds: $\left(\dfrac{557}{\quad}\right) \times 60 =$ _____ **WPM**

Comprehension Score: _____

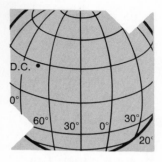

HOW TO READ IN MATHEMATICS

Two skills necessary for reading mathematics material are figuring out the pronunciations of new terms and understanding the explanations of these terms. Other skills you need in this area are reading and understanding signs, diagrams, and abbreviations.

Using so many different skills at once may seem complicated. One trick that helps make complicated material easier to understand is to visualize, or see in your mind, what the author is describing. As an example, try this simple exercise. Visualize the following directions in your mind. *Do not use paper.*

1. Draw a circle.
2. Draw a line from top to bottom, cutting the circle in half.
3. Draw a bigger circle around the first circle.
4. Draw a square around the bigger circle.

Using this method will help you to read the next selection.

Another help is to think about which reading skills are appropriate for each individual situation as you read. One sentence may require you to read new words, the next may have abbreviations in it, and the next after that may refer to a diagram somewhere else on the page. If you concentrate on using the specific reading skills you have been practicing, you will find that you can make sense even out of material that appears very complex at first.

As you read the following article, think about the skills you are using, and try to visualize what the author is writing about. Pay special attention to the word helps and diagrams.

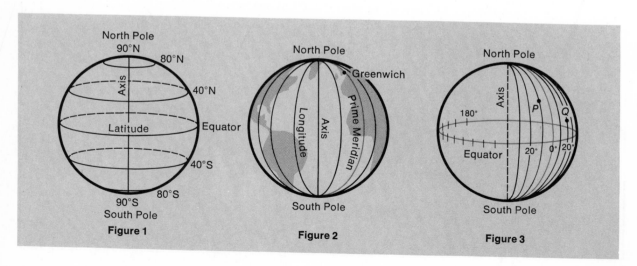

Figure 1

Figure 2

Figure 3

A sphere is a three-dimensional round figure whose surface is equally distant from the center at all points. A basketball is a sphere. The stars, moon, and planets are all spherical in shape.

A sphere with a map of the earth on it is called a globe. You have probably noticed that globes have lines going around them and lines going from top to bottom. These are called lines of latitude and longitude, and they are useful in locating places on the earth's surface. The following selection explains more about latitude and longitude.

The Earth as a Sphere _____

Written for this book
by William L. Schaaf.

We often speak of our earth as a sphere, but it is not quite a perfect sphere in shape. Not only is the surface irregular because of mountains and valleys, but the earth is also a little flatter at the poles.

The North and South Poles are the ends of an imaginary line through the center of the earth, called the earth's axis. This axis is perpendicular to an imaginary plane through the center of the earth which intersects the earth's surface in a great circle called the *equator*. (See Figure 1.) The equator divides the earth into two hemispheres (half-spheres)—the Northern Hemisphere, above the equator, and the Southern Hemisphere, below the equator.

If we imagine the earth cut by a set of planes parallel to the plane of the equator, the circles formed will be small circles of the sphere. We call them *parallels of latitude* and use them to measure the earth in a north-south direction. We number them from zero degrees (0°) at the equator to 90° at the North Pole, and again from 0° at the equator to 90° at the South Pole. (See Figure 1.)

Now consider the earth's axis once more. A set of planes can be passed through the length of the axis, and in each case the

---

perpendicular (pĕr'pen di'cū lĕr), at right angles, like the two lines of the letter *T*.

plane (plān), a flat or level surface.

intersect (in tēr sekt'), to cut across, or divide by passing through.

great circle, a circle traced on the surface of a sphere by a plane which passes through the center of the sphere.

parallel (pa'rə lel), extending in the same direction and always at the same distance apart, like the opposite sides of a square.

small circle, a circle traced on the surface of a sphere by a plane which passes through the sphere, but not through the center.

Greenwich (Gren'ich), a city near London, England.

intersection with the sphere is a great circle which passes through both the North and South Poles. Each half (from North Pole to South Pole) of one of these great circles is called a *meridian of longitude*. We use meridians to measure the earth's east-west directions. (See Figure 2.)

For convenience, one particular meridian has been selected as a starting point. It is called the *Prime Meridian*. It is the meridian which passes through Greenwich, England. The great circle of the Prime Meridian divides the earth into the Eastern Hemisphere and the Western Hemisphere. As you look at Figure 2, you can see part of the Eastern Hemisphere to the right of the Prime Meridian, and an even larger part of the Western Hemisphere to the left of the Prime Meridian.

Each half of the equator is divided into 180 equal parts by meridians of longitude which are numbered from 0° to 180°. The Prime Meridian is 0°. All the other meridians are either longitude east or longitude west of Greenwich. Thus, point *P* is on longitude 10° West; point *Q* is on longitude 20° East. (See Figure 3.)

We can describe the location of any place on the earth's surface by telling the meridian of longitude and the parallel of latitude at which the place appears on the globe. For example, Washington, D.C., is located at about 77 degrees longitude in the Western Hemisphere, and about 39 degrees latitude in the Northern Hemisphere. (See Figure 4.) This description may be abbreviated as follows: long. 77°W, lat. 39°N.

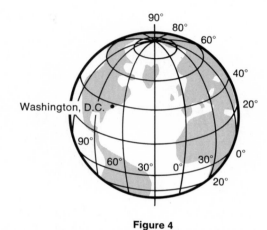

Figure 4

ACTIVITY 1

Complete the Sentences

On a separate sheet of paper, write the word that belongs in the blank in each of the sentences that follow. (You will find all the information you need in the article you just read.)

1. The earth's axis extends from the _____ to the _____.

2. All parallels of _____ are parallel to the equator.

3. The _____ is the only parallel of latitude that is a great circle.

4. Parallels of latitude measure distances on the earth's surface in a _____-_____ direction.

5. Meridians of _____ are perpendicular to the equator.

6. All meridians of longitude are great _____.

7. Meridians of longitude measure distances on the earth's surface in an _____-_____ direction.

ACTIVITY 2 — Finding Latitude and Longitude

For this activity, you will need a map of the United States, or a globe.

Using this map or globe, find the approximate latitude and longitude of each of these cities. Write the name of the city and the latitude and longitude on your paper.

1. Miami, Florida
2. St. Paul, Minnesota
3. Knoxville, Tennessee
4. Boston, Massachusetts
5. Milwaukee, Wisconsin

ACTIVITY 3 — Finding the City

Use the same map or globe you used in Activity 2 to find what large city is found at each of these locations.

On your paper, write the latitude, longitude, and name of the city.

1. 41°N, 74°W.

2. 33°N, 97°W.

3. 34°N, 118°W.

4. 40°N, 105°W.

5. 30°N, 90°W.

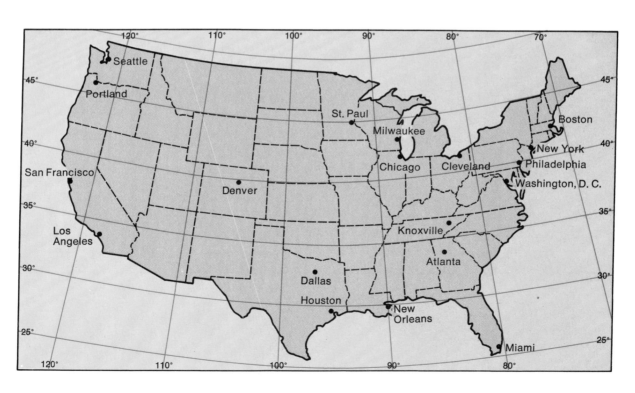

Relating Sentences to Topics

Below you will find some facts about Utah. The Pony Express route which you will read about in Unit Six passed through Utah. The mountains and deserts in this part of the trip were very difficult for the riders to cross. You will want to find out more about Utah before reading the next unit.

Three topics are given in the following boxes. There are several numbered sentences that belong to each topic. Number your paper from 2 to 20. After the number of each sentence write the letter of the topic to which the sentence belongs. The first one is done for you.

A. Surface   B. Farming   C. Mining

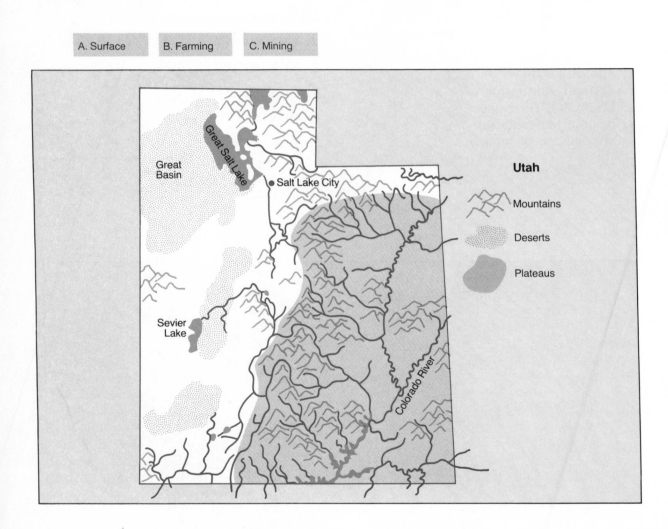

1. Ⓐ Utah is divided into two great regions.

2. Some of the farm products of Utah are wheat, oats, hay, cotton, potatoes, and sugar beets.

3. Among the nonmetal products, coal and salt take the lead in the mining industry of Utah.

4. No farming was done in Utah in early times because of the high mountains and desert regions.

5. The regions on the east are covered with high mountains and plateaus.

6. About one tenth of Utah is now used for farming purposes.

7. Mining is one of the most important industries of Utah.

8. The mountains in this eastern region reach heights of 10,000 to 13,500 feet (3,000 to 4,050 meters).

9. Every mountain range is underlaid with minerals.

10. The Great Basin was once entirely covered by a sea.

11. After a time farmers began to irrigate the land to make it possible to grow crops.

12. The other region is the Great Basin on the west.

13. Of lesser importance are its iron and zinc mines.

14. In the southern part, oranges, lemons, and figs are grown.

15. Salt, of course, is mined from the Great Salt Lake.

16. Silver is found in nearly all of the mountains.

17. The chief fruits grown in Utah are apples, peaches, plums, cherries, and grapes.

18. Gold, copper, and lead are other important metals mined in Utah.

19. Rivers formed by melting snow come leaping and foaming down their sides.

20. They found that the soil that can be watered is rich and will grow good crops when properly irrigated.

Prefixes and Suffixes

Working with Prefixes

Some more prefixes are *in*—into, not; *circum*—around; *ex*—out of, from.

Choose the correct prefix to make the word that fits each meaning below. Write the word on your paper.

1. _____ port: to send out of the port
2. _____ navigate: to sail around
3. _____ accurate; not accurate
4. _____ expensive: not high priced
5. _____ scribe: to draw a line around
6. _____ ability: state of not having ability

Working with Suffixes

Some new suffixes are *al*—pertaining to; *ward*—toward, in the direction of; *able*—able to be, or, tending toward.

Choose the correct suffix to make the word that fits each meaning below. Write the word on your paper.

1. mathematic _____: pertaining to mathematics
2. west _____: toward the west
3. home _____: toward home
4. music _____: pertaining to music
5. understand _____: able to be understood
6. change _____: able to be changed
7. peace _____: tending toward peace
8. sea _____: toward the sea

Combining Words

Here are the meanings of some words and bases that are combined to make long words. Study the meanings of these words and bases.

Base or Word	Derived from	Meaning	Where Often Used
tele	a Greek word	far, at a distance	first part of a word
1. scope	a Greek word	view, viewer	last part of word
2. phone	a Greek word	sound	last part of word
3. graph	a Greek word	something that writes	last part of word
4. vision	a Latin word	power of seeing	separate word or last part of word

On your paper combine the base *tele* with each of the other bases in the first column to make a word. Tell the meaning of each of these new words, as derived from the meaning of each of its parts.

Working with Science Words

The words below are in nearly all science textbooks at your level. You will be able to read better in the science books that you use, if you can pronounce all of these words correctly, and if you understand their meanings as used in science.

---

heredity (hə red′ə tē), inheritance of characteristics from parents.

immunization (im mū nə zā′shən), production of antibodies to protect against disease.

insecticide (in sek′tə sīd), a preparation used in killing insects.

parasite (par′ə sīt), a plant or animal living in or on another organism.

planetarium (plan′ə tār′ē əm), a building in which a projector throws lights on the ceiling to represent stars.

pollination (pol′ə nā′shən), supplying a flower with pollen to fertilize it.

radar (rā′där), a device to determine the location of an object by the reflection of radio waves.

seismograph (sīz′mə graf), an instrument which detects and records earthquakes.

turbine (tėr′bən), a machine run by steam or water which produces electrical energy. Many hundreds of electric plants are run by turbines.

uranium (ū rā′nē əm), a heavy, white, metallic, radioactive element found in rock. The pure metal is used in releasing atomic energy.

See if you know the meaning of each of these words as it is used in science. On your paper, write the word that belongs in each blank space. Add *s* if necessary.

1. One of the scientists in an observatory knew there had been an earthquake in the South Sea Islands by reading the _____ .

2. John used an _____ to kill the beetles which were destroying the rose bushes.

3. An insect that lives on a plant, and gets its food from the plant, is called a _____ .

4. When bees carry pollen from one flower to another, it is called _____ .

5. Electric power plants use _____ run by steam or water to produce electric energy.

6. If you want to study the stars, a good place to go is a _____ , where the sky is represented on the ceiling.

7. The color of your eyes is determined by the characteristics of your parents, or your _____ .

8. Even in very bad weather the location of an airplane can be determined by the reflection of radio waves transmitted by _____ .

9. All children should receive _____ against polio.

10. Many miners these days are searching for deposits of _____ , a radioactive metal found in rock.

Working with Social Studies Words

The words below have to do with the future. Study their pronunciations and meanings.

---

future shock (fū′chēr shäk), the stress people feel when they go through too much change in too short a time.

robot (rō′bət), a machine made to look and work like a human.

cyborg (sī′bôrg), a fusion of man and machine into one working unit.

cryogenics (krī′ə jen′iks), the process of freezing bodies in hopes of bringing them back to life at a future date.

cloning (klōn′ing), a reproduction of an off-spring from a single parent, producing an exact copy of the parent.

hologram (hōl′ə gram), a three-dimensional picture which makes an image look like reality.

space probe (spās prōb), any vehicle sent into outer space to report back information on conditions encountered.

space station (spās stā′shən), place in space where future spaceships will stop to take on supplies and undergo maintenance.

interstellar travel (in′tēr stel′ēr trav′l), travel between the stars.

module (mäj′ool), one of a packaged assembly of related parts which can be put together to build something.

This story takes place in the future, a hundred years from now. Finish it by finding the word above which fits best in the sentence. On your paper, write the correct words in numerical order. (Add *s* if necessary.)

I've been chosen to go on the next spaceflight, and I'm really excited. Travel between the stars, or (1) _____, isn't new, but it's the first time I've gone.

We have learned what to expect on the stars by sending up spaceships without people aboard. We learn a lot from these (2) _____. The first flights were made by (3) _____, machines that look and work like humans.

Our spaceship was built from identical sections, or (4) _____, which fit together like building blocks. Halfway to the star, we will stop at a (5) _____ to get fuel and supplies. We'll talk to people back on Earth through the use of images that look as if they're right in the spaceship with us. They're actually no more real than a TV picture. They're called (6) _____.

Let me tell you about the other members of the crew. Two of them look exactly alike. One was produced from the other through (7) _____. Another crew member is a (8) _____. His mind is human, but his body is a machine. Another man used to live in the twentieth century—a hundred years ago. Through (9) _____, he was frozen and brought back to life a few years ago. He says he can't believe how quickly things have changed since he was frozen. I'm afraid he may be suffering from (10) _____.

LIQUID TELEPHONE

"Mr. Watson, come here; I want you!" These words, the first articulate sentence ever spoken over the telephone, were uttered by Alexander Graham Bell. He spilled on his clothes some sulphuric acid part of the transmission apparatus. It was the March 10, 1876. The receiver was a tuned reed.

1876 "My ... Dom Pedro of Brazil ear ... the receiver of this ear ... Centennial Exposition. O ... Thomson (later Lord Kelvin ... most wonderful thing in Amer ...

1878 People often became confused by using the same device for talking and listening, so a new feature was added — a second wooden transmitter-receiver. You could use either for talking or listening, but you didn't have to move the instrument from mouth to ear. The crank was turned to generate power to signal the operator.

WALL SET

18 ... phon ... an e ... This emph ... Edis ...

MAGNETO WALL SET

This handsome instrument, encased in oak ... Blake transmitter and Bell's hand receiver, ... telephone built for the Bell System by West- ... side-winder models on which you turned the ... al the operator.

1886 **LONG DISTANCE TRANSMITTER** The search for better ways of transmitting the voice led to the development of this model which used a platinum diaphragm for better long distance transmission. The instrument shown in this picture actually was used by Bell and later by Theodore N. Vail, organizing genius of the Bell System.

1892 An early effort to ma ... decorative as well as more comp ... souvenir of the Gay Nineties. Th ... becoming less unwieldy, the rec ... its size so that it was called a "wa ... the ornate base reflects the taste ...

DESK

1897 **DESK SET** In the early '90s the telephone began to assume the shape in which it was to become familiar to Americans for the next three or four decades. This ancestor of the upright desk set was made in 1897 and represented a refinement of earlier similar models. It was made of cast brass.

... more ... in this ... mitter is ... reduced ... ver and

1900 **COMMON BATTERY** The effort to make telephoning more convenient is perpetual. The early telephones were voice-powered. Then a wet battery was used which, though an improvement, sometimes resulted in acid on the carpet. Dry batteries came next. The fourth stage was the common battery, with the power supply at the exchange.

190 ... phone ... rent fo ... telephon ... the '30 ... enclose

... pedestal desk ... in 1910 though ... dates back to the ... ones were made of cast

1913 **WALL SET** The wall telephone is becoming more compact. Instruments like these were in general service and were also forerunners of today's Home Interphone System. They provided intercommunication within the home and

1919 **DIAL TELE** The first dial telephone ... to Almon B. Strowger who introd ... Indiana, in 1892. It was many ye ... switching equipment was sufficiently ...

... edited ... aPorte, ... before ... permit

1928 **DESK SET** America got a new look in telephones in 1927 when the combined receiver and transmitter idea, used since 1878 by telephone linesmen, was sufficiently improved to be adapted for general service. It was popu-

1930 **DESK SET** This telephone like the 1928 se ... or without dial and resembled its predecessor e ... instead of a round base it had an elliptical or ova ... Within a few years after its introduction, it was

TELEPHONE KEY SET

... an early model of a widely used ... with one "hold" button and five others ... ling or access to other extensions. Dur- ... quarter of a century of service, this type ... s proved very useful for both internal ... munications.

1949 **"500" TYPE DESK SET** First in the new "500" series, which later would include a variety of colors. Rugged and functional, the "500" is the most commonly used telephone in the United States today. Standard with all the sets in this series is an adjustable volume control for the bell located in the base of the telephone.

1954 **"500" TYPE COU** In 1954 the telephone ... decorative household item. Although ... phones were available much earlier ... widespread popularity until the adve ... series. The five basic colors currently ... beige, green, pink and blue.

... me a ... d tel- ... t gain ... color ... white,

1956 **WALL TELEPHONE** The telephone returns to the wall in this companion piece to the "500" desk set. Designed for convenience, the wall set is most often used in the kitchen where counter and table space is at a premium. It is also popular in such areas as basements, garages, and covered patios. Colors: White, beige, yellow, and pink.

1958 **SPEAKERPHONE SET** Microphone and speaker units free the user's hands to make notes or look up reference material. It also permits conference conversations between groups at different locations. If privacy is desired, it may be used as a conventional telephone. Colors: White, beige, green, gray, pink and blue.

1 ... tions. ... several ... same tim ... button or ... or speak

PRINCESS® TELEPHONE

... little, it's lovely, it lights ..." The desk ... ew look. Compactness, attractive styling ... al lit lights up when you lift the handset

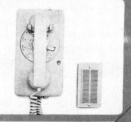

1960 **HOME INTERPHONE SYSTEM** An outgrowth of the inter-commu ... services offered to businesses for many year ... INTERPHONE service employs specially eq

TELEPHONE

... mmunications, the ... button is pressed, ... ated and trans

1968 **TOUCH-TONE® TRIMLINE® TELEPHONE** Latest in the line of telephones is the 12 button Touch-Tone Trimline set which combines hand-set and pushbuttons in one lightweight unit. Although

196 ... newest in ... Pictures

**HOW TO READ
LITERATURE**

So far in this book you have been reading stories that are written in the usual way. They have been written in regular paragraph form, with some description and some speaking by the characters.

But stories do not have to be written this way. The next story you will read is different. It is a combination of letters and telephone conversations. In some ways it is somewhat like a play, and you might read it as you would a play. Try to imagine how the characters are speaking. What tone of voice might they be using? Where might they be sitting or standing? How might the other character react to what the speaker is saying? What expression might be on a character's face as she is reading a letter?

Think about those questions as you read the story. They will help you make the characters come alive in your mind.

At some time or other almost everyone has a misunderstanding with someone he or she is close to. How do such misunderstandings come about? How do the people involved feel? What can be done to straighten out the misunderstanding and avoid others in the future? The next story will suggest some answers to these questions and help you learn more about human communications.

"But You Said . . ." _____

Written for this book
by Irene Elmer.

January 15

Dear Heather,

It's weird not having you around here anymore after we lived next door to each other for six years. How are things at your new school and what are you doing? Things are okay here, and I'm in three classes with Margo Fitzsimmons, that red-haired girl who's on the judo team. Remember her? She makes judo sound great, and I think I may take it myself this year. I can't wait until I see you this summer—don't forget, that's when we're going camping!

Love,
Jan

January 25

Dear Jan,

Hi. Thanks for your note. Now that I'm used to this place I really like it, though it was slightly weird at first, entering in the middle of the year the way I did. You go into this huge school—there are 3,000 people staring at you and you don't know a soul— you think, "Ye gods! What am I doing here?" But they have a drama club, so I joined it right away, and already I'm involved in a project. You know me— never happy unless I'm impossibly overworked. Hope things are going okay with you.

Love,
Heather

gi (gē), pajama-like clothing worn in judo.

katate tori (kä tä′tē tō′rē), a one-handed hold used in judo.

February 10

JAN: Hi, Heather, it's me, Jan. Hey, I'll bet you didn't expect me to phone you long distance.

HEATHER: Jan, how marvelous to hear from you! Why are you calling?

JAN: Oh, I just sort of felt like it, and I happen to be temporarily rich. How's the acting going?

HEATHER: Fantastic! I tried out for a part in *The Importance of Being Earnest*, and I'm waiting now to see if I get it; that's what I thought it was when the phone rang.

JAN: Sorry.

HEATHER: Oh, that's okay. How's the judo going?

JAN: Great, I love it; of course I'm only a beginner, but Margo says I should think about trying out for the team next year.

HEATHER: I'll bet you're good at it. Do you wear one of those pajama things?

JAN: A gi—yes. (*After a pause*) Well, it's been great talking to you, Heather, but I guess I'd better hang up before my money runs out. Listen—I'm really looking forward to our camping trip this summer.

HEATHER: To what? Oh, the camping trip. (*Politely*) Sure, so am I, Jan. Well, glad you called.

March 2

Heather,

It's about time we started getting our camping trip organized. What would you think of going to Badger Pass? Tell your mother my parents will give me permission to go provided we stay at the Y lodge. There's great hiking on the glacier beds.

Love,
Jan

March 24

Heather,

Haven't heard from you since I wrote you about going to Badger Pass. I wrote to the Y lodge. Reservations for summer are going fast, so I made tentative reservations for the week of June 12—okay?

Jan

April 8

HEATHER: Hello? Oh, Jan. Hi. How are you?

JAN: Fine. Hey, didn't you get my last two postcards?

HEATHER: Yes, I got them.

JAN: Well, what about it? Is Badger Pass okay with you? The lodge isn't bad, you know. It's kind of quaint and rustic, and there are some nice, strenuous hikes.

HEATHER (*after a pause*): Okay.

JAN: Hey, you sure don't sound too enthusiastic. Is there some other place you'd rather go?

HEATHER (*after a pause*): No. If we're going camping, then any place you want is fine with me.

JAN (*astonished*): What do you mean, *if* we're going camping?

HEATHER: Well, naturally, if you *want* to go . . .

JAN: Sure I want to go; it'll be great. So, what have you been doing? Did you get the part you wanted in that play?

HEATHER: *The Importance of Being Earnest*—yes, I got it. We're in rehearsal now. Listen, Jan, I have to hang up now.

JAN: Okay. Nice talking to you, Heather.

April 14

Dear Heather,

I confirmed our reservations for the week of June 12. The lodge people say the weather should be pretty good by then, but that we can expect a few squalls, maybe some snow. I told them a little snow wouldn't bother us. Margo says she's jealous (she's kidding—she's really neat, and you'd love her). She does a lot of hiking. Of course, judo's her specialty, and she's really been teaching me a lot. I learned to do *katate tori* the other day—that's where you put a flex and twist on your opponent's arm. I'll show you how to do it when I see you.

Love,
Jan

May 12

Dear Jan,

I'm sorry, but I won't be able to make it in June. I thought I told you, we're putting on *Earnest* at the Civic Theatre right after school lets out. Of course we were incredibly lucky to get the chance, and there's no way I could back out now. I'm really crushed. I just wish you'd informed me before you made the reservations.

Heather

May 16

JAN: Heather? Is that you? Listen, what do you mean you can't make it in June?

HEATHER: I told you, that's when we're putting on *Earnest*.

JAN (angrily): But that's when we agreed we were going camping.

HEATHER: I never said for sure that I was going, if you'll recall.

JAN (outraged): If you didn't want to go, why didn't you say so in the first place?

HEATHER: Anybody could see I didn't want to. If you weren't so insensitive . . . !

JAN: How was I supposed to know? You *said* you wanted to.

HEATHER: I thought *you* wanted to. I was only trying to cooperate.

JAN (yelling): Cooperate? Ha!

HEATHER (yelling): Listen, if you want to slog around in the snow and learn to break people's arms, that's fine with me. It just so happens I have better things to do!

JAN (yelling): Well, do them, then! Be my guest! (*She slams down the receiver and bursts into tears.*)

May 23

Dear Jan,

I'm sorry about our misunderstanding. I think what happened was that we didn't communicate properly. I never really told you how I felt, and maybe you didn't listen too well, either. Phone me collect when you get this, and let's discuss it.

Love,
Heather

May 28

HEATHER: . . . So, let me tell you what I learned about communication. You can't just *sort of* say something and hope the other person gets it. You have to say exactly what you mean, and say it clearly, so that the other person *understands*. And the person who is listening really has to listen. Sometimes it helps to have the other person repeat back what you said, so you can tell if he or she understood you. (*After*

a pause) So, first I would say to you that I don't really want to go camping, but I still want to be friends. And you would say . . .

JAN: Wait; then I say, "I understand you don't want to go camping, but you do want to be friends"—right? That's okay with me, Heather. Listen, I'll tell you what. I'm going camping with Margo instead of you. On our way back, what if we dropped by to say hello? You could meet Margo, and maybe we could come and see you in that play.

HEATHER: Fantastic. I'd like that, Jan. Then you can demonstrate some judo, and I'll watch you—from a distance.

1

ACTIVITY

Fact Questions

1. What new sport was Jan learning?

2. What was the name of Jan's new friend?

3. At what point in the year did Heather enter her new school?

4. What club did Heather join at her new school?

5. What was the name of the area where Jan wanted to go camping?

6. Under what conditions would Jan's parents allow her to go camping?

7. For what date did she plan the trip?

8. Why did Heather say she couldn't go?

9. What did Heather say a speaker should do in order to communicate properly?

10. What did Heather say a listener should do?

ACTIVITY 2

Thought Questions

1. Heather uses expressions like "slightly weird," "ye gods," "impossibly over-worked," and "really crushed." What does her choice of words tell you about Heather?

2. Do you think Jan or Heather contributed more to their misunderstanding? Why?

3. Find all the places where Heather avoids telling Jan how she really feels.

What does she do instead? How could she communicate more clearly?

4. Find all the places where Jan takes Heather's wishes or feelings for granted, or where she doesn't stop to listen carefully. How does this cause problems in their communication?

5. Why do you think Heather doesn't tell Jan how she really feels about camping?

6. Do you think Heather and Margo will like each other? If they had met before the things in this story happened, would they have liked each other more than they will now? Less? Why?

7. Will Jan and Heather still be friends a year from now? Explain your answer.

ACTIVITY 3

Thinking About Literature

1. In the telephone conversations, how can you tell who is speaking?

2. What helps you know how the characters are speaking?

3. Find the only place where you are told the actions of a character. How are the actions described?

**HOW TO READ IN
SOCIAL STUDIES**

The next selection you will read is about the history of the Pony Express. This selection has several numbers in it. It will be a good one for you to use in getting more practice in the skill of scanning.

1. Suppose that you are interested only in finding out the *dates* of important events which happened just before, during, and immediately after the life of the Pony Express. Try to glance straight down through the middle of the page quickly, pausing only when you catch sight of a date. When you do see a date, stop long enough to find what event took place on that date, and try to impress both the date and the event on your mind. Then scan the page until you catch a glimpse of another date. Find out the event that took place on that date, and try to think of the second date in relation to the first one, perhaps estimating how many years elapsed between the two. Continue in this way, scanning for and thinking about the dates in the selection until the entire selection has been covered.

    When you have finished scanning the selection for dates, do Activity 1.

2. After finishing with your scanning, read the last three paragraphs of the selection carefully. You will be asked some reasoning questions about statements made in these paragraphs.

In the story about Jan and Heather, much of the misunderstanding occurred through letters. Later, the girls were able to clear up their troubles by talking about them directly. But there was a time when letters were the only way people could communicate over great distances. And letters traveled much more slowly in those days. The next article will tell you more about how the mail was delivered in the last century.

History of the Pony Express _____

Written for this book
by Wallace E. Lamb.

Before the time of the Pony Express, the growing settlements on the Pacific Coast were shut off from the rest of the nation. Separating California from the Mississippi River were 2,000 miles (3,200 kilometers) of desert and mountains. There was a great need for providing better communication.

Up to that time, the best way was to send mail from New York to San Francisco by boat. Some of the mail boats sailed all around South America by Cape Horn. Others went by way of Panama. At that time there was no canal at Panama. The mail was taken off one boat, carried across the Isthmus by mules, and then loaded on another boat.

The first mail to go overland to California arrived in Los Angeles in May 1848. Several weeks were required for a letter to go from the East to California. Twenty-five days were required for mail to be carried by stagecoach from Missouri to California. Further delays might be caused by mud, high water, snow, or bandits. It was very important that some better means of communication be found.

Finally, the Pony Express was organized. The plan was to send mail by fast horses instead of by stagecoach. The route was to run from St. Joseph, Missouri, to Sacramento, California.

On April 3, 1860, the Pony Express service began. On that day, a train from the East brought mail into St. Joseph. At four o'clock that afternoon, Henry Wallace, the first rider of the Pony Express, galloped westward on a fast pony. After riding twenty-five miles, he changed to a second pony, and after fifty miles to a third. After seventy-five miles he was replaced by another rider who was waiting to continue on a fourth fresh pony. At the same time another rider jumped into the saddle at Sacramento and started galloping east. The average speed of the ponies was about 8 miles (12.8 kilometers) per hour. Later, mail carried by the Pony Express traveled about 240 miles (384 kilometers) per day in each direction.

The route of the Pony Express passed through the wildest part of the country.

---

communication (kə mū′nə kā′shən), any exchange of information and ideas by speaking, writing, telegraph, etc.

isthmus (is′məs), a narrow strip of land connecting two larger land masses; the narrow strip of land, known as Panama which connects North and South America.

receipts (ri sēts′), money received in return for a product or service.

tradition (trə dish′ən), an ideal or standard of behavior handed down from earlier times.

Main Street, Salt Lake City

The only settlement along the entire route, except for a few army posts, was at Salt Lake City. The company placed many stations along the way. The station keepers kept watch for approaching riders and had fresh ponies ready. But sometimes bandits raided their stations, killed the keepers, and stole the horses. A rider, dashing into such a station, would find no rider to relieve him and no fresh horse. He usually had to continue onward as best he could.

The Pony Express was big business. In all, it had 190 stations, 80 riders, about 400 horses, and over 400 station keepers and helpers. At first the charge for mail delivery was $5.00 per half ounce, but this was later reduced to $1.00. Receipts for a single trip could run as high as $1,000. At first there was one trip per week. After June 1860, there were two trips each week. The time was shortened from ten days to eight. As a public service the Pony Express was a great success, but it did not make money. It ended up with a debt of $200,000.

Meanwhile telegraph wires were being strung across the country from New York City to San Francisco. As the wires were strung west of the Mississippi, the route of the Pony Express was shortened. In October 1861, the Pony Express was finally discontinued.

Altogether, the Pony Express ran only about a year and a half. For this reason it was not of great importance in the history of the nation. But while it lasted it lived up to the finest traditions of the West. It was a successful attempt to meet the need for better communication between the East and the Pacific Coast. There was nothing that could stop the westward expansion of Americans across the United States. Within thirty years after the Pony Express, the larger part of the territory between Missouri and the Pacific was settled, and the great American frontier was closed.

ACTIVITY 1 — Dates and Events

On your paper, write the three headings below. Then fill in the dates and the events that happened on these dates as you gathered them by scanning.

Events	Year	Month
1.		
2.		
3.		
4.		

ACTIVITY 2 — Reasons

Answer these questions on your own paper.

1. The author said that the Pony Express did not make money, and that it piled up a debt of $200,000. What reasons can you give for the lack of success of the Pony Express as a business venture?

2. The author said that ". . . the Pony Express ran only about a year and a half. For this reason it was not of great importance in the history of the nation." Is his reason strong enough to warrant such a broad conclusion? Tell why you do or do not agree with him.

ACTIVITY 3

Study this picture carefully. Then write a short paragraph describing the Pony Express, using all the information that you can gather by reading the picture. Include *all* that you can read directly from the picture, but don't include anything that you can't read from the picture.

A beginning sentence for the paragraph might be: "The Pony Express route extended from St. Joseph, Missouri, to Sacramento, California."

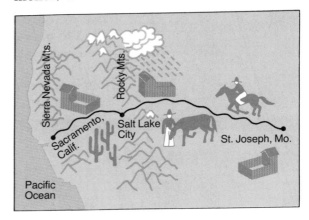

135

HOW TO READ IN SCIENCE

The next article explains how the telephone works. It is similar to the material which you find in certain parts of your science textbooks. Material of this type must be read slowly and thoughtfully.

1. Read the headings to find out what topics are discussed in the selection.
2. Study the first diagram, noticing especially the parts that are labeled.
3. After reading the introductory paragraph, read the first section to find the answer to the question "How does the transmitter work?" In working with this section, read just one sentence at a time. If it mentions something shown in the diagram, look back at the diagram after reading the sentence. When you are sure that you understand that sentence, read the next one in the same way. Stop and think about each sentence after you have read it to make sure that the meaning is clear to you.

   When you have finished reading the entire section, see if you can give the explanation to yourself in your own words. If not, go back and reread the parts that you need to make your explanation complete.
4. Work with each of the remaining sections in the same way that you worked with the first one. The third section has no diagram, but you should study it in the same way that you studied the other two sections.

1876 **LIQUID TELEPHONE**
"Mr. Watson, come here; I want you!" These historic words, the first articulate sentence ever spoken over an electric telephone, were uttered by Alexander Graham Bell when he spilled on his clothes some sulphuric acid which was part of the transmission apparatus. It was the night of March 10, 1876. The receiver was a tuned reed.

1876 **BELL'S CENTENNIAL MODEL**
"My word! It talks!" exclaimed Emperor Dom Pedro of Brazil on June 25, 1876, when he listened to the receiver of this early telephone at the Philadelphia Centennial Exposition. One of the judges, Sir William Thomson (later Lord Kelvin) called Bell's invention "the most wonderful thing in America."

One of the best ways to communicate with someone is to speak directly to that person. In that way, if a misunderstanding arises, it can be explained and discussed right away. Both people can react and respond right away. The telephone makes it possible for people to speak directly with each other even though they may be thousands of miles apart. Read the next article to find out how the telephone works.

How Does the Telephone Work?

The telephone has two parts. The *transmitter* is the part into which you speak. The *receiver* is the part which you place to your ear.

How Does the Transmitter Work?

The first thing you need to know is that when you speak, your voice sets up sound waves in the air. When you speak into the transmitter, these sound waves strike against a light-weight disk of metal called the *diaphragm*. This diaphragm is the top

---

diaphragm (dī′ə fram), a disk-like partition that vibrates.

vibrations (vī brā′shənz), rapid back and forth motions.

electromagnet (i lek′trō mag′nit), a core of soft iron surrounded by a coil of wire through which an electric current is passed to magnetize the core.

molecule (mol′ə kūl), a small particle.

electron (i lek′tron), a particle having a single charge of negative electricity.

proton (prō′ton), a particle having a single charge of positive electricity.

of a box holding tiny particles, or granules, of carbon. Look at Figure 1.

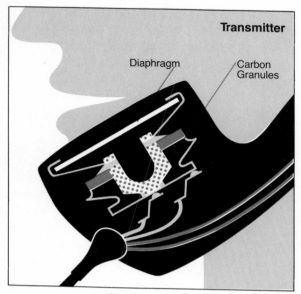

Transmitter

Diaphragm

Carbon Granules

Figure 1

When you talk on the telephone, electricity is passing through the carbon granules. Your voice controls this flow of electricity. As you speak, your voice causes the diaphragm to vibrate and to press down on the carbon granules. When you speak loudly, the vibrations are strong. They force the granules to be packed tightly together. Electricity can flow through them easily. When you speak softly, the vibrations are weak and the granules become loosely packed. Less electricity passes through them. Several changes may take place in the granules as you say each word.

The flow of electricity carries all of these changes over the wire. Now it remains for the receiver at the other end of the line to change these strong and weak variations in electricity back into sound waves like those made by your voice.

How Does the Receiver Work?

The receiver also has two important parts, another metal diaphragm and an electromagnet. An electromagnet is a metal rod wrapped in a coil of wire. When electricity passes through the wire coil, the rod becomes a magnet and pulls on the diaphragm. The pull of the magnet becomes strong or weak according to the electrical pattern sent by the transmitter. Look at Figure 2.

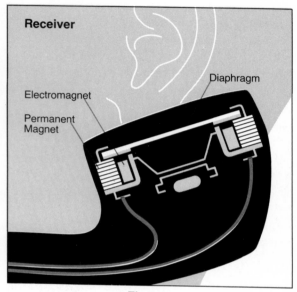

Receiver

Diaphragm

Electromagnet

Permanent Magnet

Figure 2

When the pull of the magnet is strong, the diaphragm moves toward it. When the pull weakens, the diaphragm moves away. These movements of the diaphragm occur very rapidly. They create sound waves by causing the air to vibrate.

These sound waves travel to your ear. Since they vibrate at exactly the same rate as the sound waves made by the voice of the person speaking to you, what you hear is an exact reproduction of that person's voice.

How Do Electric Wires Carry Messages?

Now you need to find out how the vibrations of your voice are carried by electricity through wires.

In order to understand this, you need to know what electricity is. You know that all materials are made up of molecules. You also know that molecules are made up of atoms. Atoms contain two kinds of charged particles—those carrying a positive electrical charge, and those carrying a negative electrical charge. The negative particles are called *electrons*. Electrons move easily. The positive particles are called *protons*. The protons are nearly 2,000 times as heavy as electrons. They do not move easily. Atoms have an equal number of electrons and protons.

An electric battery or generator destroys the balance of electrons and protons in atoms. It does this by concentrating more electrons at one of its poles than at the other. This pole then has a negative charge. The other pole has a positive charge. When the poles are connected, as by a copper wire, the extra electrons at the negative pole flow along the wire toward the positive pole in order to restore the balance. This flow is called an *electric current*.

As long as the poles are connected, the balance cannot be restored. This is because the action of the electric battery or generator continues to move electrons away from the protons as fast as the electrons arrive. The path of this continuing flow is called a *circuit*.

When someone calls you on the phone, a circuit is completed as he or she dials the last digit of your number. When you pick up the phone, you keep the circuit open and allow the transmitter and receiver in each phone to function. The circuit is broken when one phone is replaced.

ACTIVITY **Listing Steps in a Process**

You will need plenty of space in doing 1, 2, and 3, so do your work on a large sheet of paper.

1. List in order the steps that take place from the time you begin to talk into the transmitter until the wires pick up the vibrations of your voice.

2. List in order the steps that take place from the time the current reaches the receiver until the person to whom you are talking hears your voice in his or her ear.

3. Explain in your own words what causes an electric current to flow. Try to do this in one paragraph.

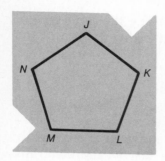

HOW TO READ IN MATHEMATICS

In this lesson you will learn the mathematics of zig-zag paths. You will need to read diagrams and a table. You will need to study the diagrams carefully in order to answer questions about them and to complete the table. Sometimes you will be reading letters, sometimes numerals. Sometimes you will be reading words in order to understand explanations and to find out what the questions are asking of you.

In addition to reading these many different kinds of symbols, you will be looking back and forth from the table to the diagrams and from questions to the diagrams. You will have to change many times from reading words to reading diagrams. In reading most lessons in mathematics, you will have to use entirely different eye movements than you use in reading a story. See how well you can do this in reading the mathematical material in this lesson.

The riders of the Pony Express made many stops, and they often traveled over zig-zag paths. Airplanes do the same thing. They even travel a zig-zag path when coming in for a landing.

Paths, Points, and Polygons _____

Written for this book
by William L. Schaaf.

We can represent the route of an airplane by a diagram, where each dot stands for an airport.

San Francisco   St. Louis

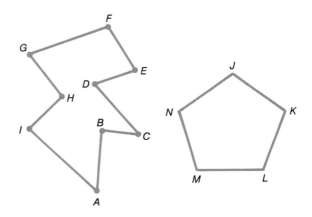

We call this diagram a *path*. Each dot is called a *vertex* (plural: *vertices*). Each connecting segment is a side. Do you see that in such an open path the number of sides is always one less than the number of vertices?

If a path returns to the point at which it started, it is a closed path. In mathematics this path is called a *polygon* (*ABCDEF-GHI*). If all the sides are equal, and all the interior angles are equal, it is a *regular polygon* (*JKLMN*).

A line connecting any two vertices of a polygon that are not immediate neighbors is called a *diagonal* of the polygon. When a regular polygon is drawn, together with all its diagonals, the result is said to be the *complete graph* of the polygon. Here are some complete graphs. Do you see that in each case every *pair* of vertices is connected?

| 3 Vertices = Triangle | 4 Vertices = Square | 5 Vertices = Pentagon | 6 Vertices = Hexagon | 7 Vertices = Heptagon |

network (net′wŭrk′), any system of lines that cross at regular intervals.

vertex (vĕr′teks), the point where two sides of an angle meet.

1

ACTIVITY

Answer these questions on your own paper.

1. In a polygon, how does the number of sides compare with the number of vertices?

2. A fence along a straight road is 120 meters long. If the fence posts are 2 meters apart, how many posts are there?

3. A board 8 meters long is sawed into pieces each 2 meters long. How many pieces are there? How many cuts must be made?

4. Study this table and compare it with the regular polygons on page 141. In the table, V represents the number of vertices (and also the number of sides). M is the number of diagonals from each vertex. The formula for the total number of diagonals is $d = \frac{1}{2}M \times V$. The formula for the total number of segments is $V + d$. Copy and complete this table.

V	M	M × V	$d = \frac{1}{2}M \times V$	V + d
3	0	0	0	3
4	1	4	2	6
5	2	10	5	10
6	3	18	9	15
7	4	28	14	
8	5			
9	6			
10	7			

I DON'T CARE WHAT YOU CALL IT. A POLYGON IS STILL A POLYGON.

Critical Reading: One Picture Is Worth a Thousand Words

You know how pictures can help you understand difficult reading material. But have you ever thought about how much can be learned from just a picture alone—and a simple picture at that?

Good communication is never easy, but for travelers, communication sometimes presents special problems. More and more people are traveling to foreign countries for business or pleasure. Often, travelers do not speak the language of every country they may visit. That's where pictures come in. In 1975, the Department of Transportation began a test using signs with pictures instead of words as an aid to travelers who may not speak or read English. If the signs are successful, they may be adopted for use throughout the world.

Here are some of these signs that are being placed in railroad stations and airports. They will direct people to places where they can get their baggage weighed, mail a letter, or ask about a hotel room. Number your paper from 1 to 8. Next to each number, write the letter of the sign that would help.

1. first aid
2. general information
3. ticket window
4. no smoking

5. mail box
6. hotel information
7. lost and found
8. baggage

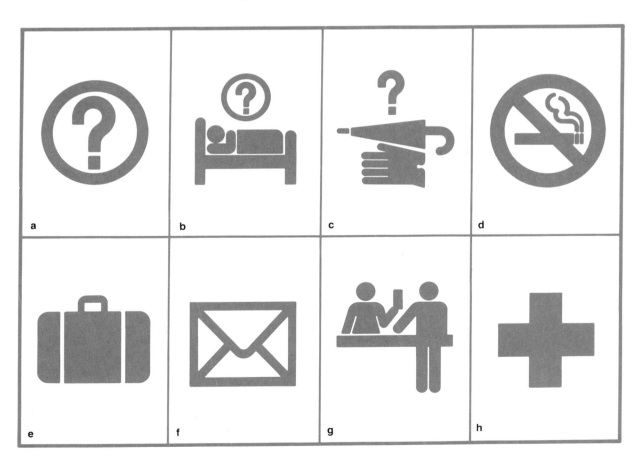

Using an Encyclopedia _____

Among your reference books, encyclopedias are the most exciting. Encyclopedias contain information about every topic in the world—and even in the universe.

Have you learned the short cuts in using an encyclopedia? Can you find items quickly?

No matter how well you think you can use an encyclopedia, you can always improve. Additional practice is given to you at this point. See how fast you can follow the directions and answer the questions at the same time making certain that each answer is correct.

The subjects in an encyclopedia are arranged in alphabetical order. In most encyclopedias, several volumes are needed to contain all the information. Each volume has a letter or group of letters on its spine to tell you that subjects beginning with that letter or group of letters will be found in that particular volume. The volumes are numbered in order.

A set of encyclopedias is pictured here. Write on your paper the number of the volume in which each of these topics would be found. See how quickly you can work.

1. birds
2. India
3. Texas
4. whales
5. glass
6. electricity

7. flags
8. diamond
9. snakes
10. Africa
11. cattle
12. Japan

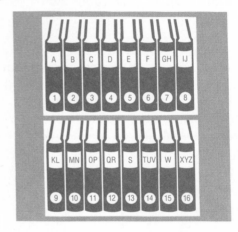

_____

That was easy because there was just one word to look up. If there are two or more words in a topic, you have to decide which word to look up.

If you wish to look up a person other than royalty you look for the last name. In looking up Edward Gordon Craig, you would find this name listed in the *C* volume as *Craig, Edward Gordon.* In the case of royalty, you look for the first name. If you were looking for George IV of the House of Hanover, you would look under *G* for *George.*

Other topics with more than one word are listed under the first of the two words. North Dakota is listed under *North,* and New Jersey is listed under *New.*

See how quickly you can write on your paper the number of the volume in which you would find each of the topics below.

1. Thomas Jefferson
2. Yosemite Valley
3. Johann Sebastian Bach
4. United States government
5. first aid
6. American Revolution
7. Olympic Games

8. Articles of Confederation
9. Elizabeth II, Queen of Great Britain
10. Madame Curie
11. Willie Mays
12. Franklin Delano Roosevelt
13. Samuel Morse
14. Pony Express

Finding Causes and Effects

Much of your reading in social studies and science deals with causes and effects. If you can quickly grasp causes and effects, you will be greatly helped in studying these subjects.

You will be given practice on this page in finding causes and effects.

Causes and Effects

In these paragraphs, causes are given which lead up to some effect. Find the cause in each paragraph and on your paper sum it up in a few words with the label *Cause*. Then find the effect and sum it up in a few words with the label *Effect*.

1. There was a time when great ice sheets from the Arctic region swept down over the northern part of the United States. These great ice sheets changed the contour of the land. As they swept along, they carried rocks and gravel in front of them. Often they scooped out great cavities in the earth. The Great Lakes and the many smaller lakes in Michigan, Wisconsin, and Minnesota were formed by the sweeping movement of these gigantic sheets of ice.

2. The soils in many of our dry lands are rich, but they cannot grow crops. Growing plants need water. When water is brought in through pipes and ditches, crops grow very well. Irrigation has made deserts bloom.

3. There are heavy forests in the tropical regions, but getting logs out of these forests is a difficult problem. The ground is water-soaked, there are few railroads or highways, and most of the logs are too heavy to float on the streams. Because of these reasons, very little logging can be done in the heavy forests of the tropics.

Effects and Causes

In each of the next selections, the effect is given first. Then follows an explanation of the cause. After reading each selection, sum up and write the effect and its cause on your paper.

1. A dog turns around and around before lying down. Why does he do this?

   This habit is supposed to be inherited. The wild dog turned round and round to trample down the grass so he would have a smooth bed. Our dogs today have no need to do this. It is thought that they perform this same activity because their ancestors did.

2. When you pop corn, the small, hard kernels suddenly burst into large, soft, snow-white bodies. Why do the hard kernels undergo this change?

   There is some moisture inside of each kernel. When you hold the kernels over the fire, this moisture turns to steam. The steam bursts the outer shell of the kernel and puffs up the inner part.

3. Bird's-eye maple is beautiful and expensive wood. It has small round spots in it that look something like a bird's eyes. What causes these marks?

   The marks are the result of an injury to the bark. When the bark is injured, the trunk begins to send out weak little sprouts. Each of these sprouts becomes a center of a ring that makes the markings.

Working with Mathematics Words and Phrases ___

The words and phrases below appear in mathematics textbooks at your level. Work out the pronunciation of each word or phrase. Next study the meaning which each word or phrase has in mathematics.

---

consumer (kən soom' ēr), one who uses goods.

currency (kūr'ən sē), money in bills or coins which passes from hand to hand in buying and selling.

surtax (sūr'taks), an extra tax to be paid in addition to the regular income tax.

BONDS

bond (bond), a special kind of note stating that on a certain date the buyer will receive the face value of the bond.

maturity value (mə tūr'ə tē val'ū), the maturity value of a Series E United States Savings Bond is the original amount plus an increase in value each year for five years.

redemption value (ri demp'shən val'ū), if a Series E Savings Bond is cashed or redeemed any time before five years after purchase, you receive the original price plus interest to the time of redemption. This is called *redemption value*.

INSURANCE

annual premium (an'ū əl prē' mē əm), the amount paid each year for a contract of insurance.

insurance (in shoor'əns), a contract promising payment in case of damage, injury, or death.

policy (pol'ə sē), the insurance contract itself.

social security (sō'shəl si kūr'ə tē), a lifelong insurance and old-age pension provided by the federal government.

See if you know the meaning of each of these words as it is used in mathematics. On your paper, write the word that belongs in each blank space. Add *s* if necessary.

1. Mr. Perez paid an income tax of $3,000. In addition, he had to pay a _____ of $300.

2. If the price of wheat is reduced, the price of flour and bread should then be similarly reduced for the _____.

3. She did not write a check for the groceries. She paid with _____.

4. For one kind of United States _____ you pay $750 and after 10 years you get $1000.

5. The _____ of this bond is $1,000.

6. Mr. Hodgson had one of these bonds for which he had paid $750. He sold it after he had held it for 5 years. The _____ of the bond was $875.

7. Mr. Stewart is an old gentleman past 65 years of age. Each month he receives a _____ check for $118.

8. Mr. Medina took out life _____ for himself and his wife.

9. The company gave him one _____ for himself and one for his wife.

10. He paid an _____ of $75 for each policy each year.

Working with Literary Words

Often when you have read a story, play, or poem, you want to talk about it with your classmates and friends. You will find such discussions easier if you know the right words for talking about things in literature. Also, as you go farther on in school, you will come across many of these words in your English books or literature anthologies. Knowing what the words are and what they mean will make your reading easier and more meaningful to you.

Here are some words that you are likely to come across or want to use. Study their pronunciations and meanings.

alliteration (ə lit′ēr ā′shən), repetition of an initial sound, usually a consonant, in two or more words in a phrase or sentence.

autobiography (ô′tə bī og′rə fē), the story of one's life written by oneself.

biography (bī og′rə fē), the account of a person's life, told by another.

dialogue (dī′ə log), what is said by the characters in a story or play.

metaphor (met′ə fôr′), speaking or writing of one thing as if it were another thing (e.g., "All the world's a stage").

monologue (mon′ə log′), a part of a play or story in which one character speaks alone; a long speech by one person.

protagonist (prō tag′ə nist), the main character in a play or story.

rhyme (rīm), the matching of end sounds (e.g., *compare* and *affair*).

simile (sim′ə lē), comparing one thing to another by using *like* or *as* (e.g., "He was as white as a ghost").

villain (vil′ən), a wicked character in a play or story.

See if you know the meaning of each of these words. On your paper, write the word that belongs in each blank space.

1. When she wrote the line "Hope is the thing with feathers," Emily Dickinson was using ———.

2. In the silent movie we saw last night, the ——— tied the victim to the railroad tracks.

3. "The wild wind whistled around the windowpane" is an example of ———.

4. In the story "Something to Lose" the ——— began as a slave but fought for his freedom.

5. "My love is like a red, red rose" is a famous ——— that begins a poem by Robert Burns.

6. For English class, I have to write an ——— that begins when I was a baby and tells about my life up till now.

7. The first Pulitzer Prize ever awarded in the class of ——— was given to Laura E. Richards and Maude Howe Elliott, who wrote the life story of Julia Ward Howe.

8. The part of the play where Hamlet is alone on stage giving a ——— was very moving.

9. I think the poet chose the name *Amanda* only to ——— with *panda*.

10. The ——— between Shirley and Joyce was better than the one in which Shirley was talking to Fred.

147

7

Dollars and Sense

You already know that the conflict in a story is the problem or problems the characters face. Sometimes characters deal with their problems face to face and try to solve them directly. Other times they may try to run away from problems or avoid them by finding distraction, escape, or replacements for what they really want.

As you read the next story, think about what the conflict is and how the main character tries to deal with it. Before you begin reading, look at the questions in Activity 3. Think about these questions as you read the story.

Record your beginning and ending times.

Most people want enough money so they can have some to save and some to spend. But there are two ways to use money—foolishly and wisely. In this story, Sally uses her money to solve a conflict. See if you can tell why the first way is foolish—and why the second is wise.

Recovery

Written for this book
by Corinna Harmon.

Dear Sally,

We feel like deserters, leaving our only and favorite daughter, but we know you're in good hands with the Okin family. Your Mom still hasn't gotten over the three months in that trailer. We both know how important your swimming is, but she just couldn't take another day of it. This check is for you to spend however you want, and we'll get something to you every week. Swim a lap for us.

Love,
Dad

Sally vacuumed the floor, part of the agreement for her room and board. Her parents had been unable to adjust to Florida, but they had let her stay so she could train every day. In Vermont, they lived far from an indoor pool and Sally despised the ride home in the winter, her clothes clammy from the locker room. And then there was her parents' constant worrying that she would become ill from going out in the cold with wet hair. Indeed, last winter she had been sick with one cold after another. For Sally's sake, they had tried moving to a warmer climate.

Her bathing suit rolled in a towel, Sally jogged the few blocks to the pool. Two hours later she hauled herself out of the water.

"Great—not even out of breath, are you?" joked Mr. Busch, her coach, squatting beside her. Then he looked serious. "I told you to take off Friday and Saturday nights."

She shrugged.

"Now take this down," he said. "I want to win the state championship as much as you do. But I don't want you to turn into a hermit. Go out more often, eat some pizza, play pinball. A few extra laps will take off the few extra ounces, if that's what's worrying you."

In Vermont, Sally had done all those things. There, she had had friends. But she had come to the new school late in the year, and no one had made much of an effort to be friendly. Sally was shy about putting herself forward. What if they made fun of her different accent? What if they just didn't like her? She felt safer at the pool, where she knew she would never be a failure.

Friday afternoon, Sally took a bus to a different pool. That would be her weekend

---

hermit (hẽr′mit), a person who lives alone in a place far away from other people.

disintegrate (dis in′tə grāt′), separate into parts; break up.

pool, and it was unlikely that Mr. Busch would find out about it.

Since Sally did nothing but swim, she spent very little and the weekly checks from her parents accumulated. One day she stared at her old worn-out bathing suit hanging over the shower curtain rod. Mr. Busch had remarked that he was afraid she might burst the seams if she flexed too many muscles. It was so faded, she could hardly tell what the original color had been.

On Monday after school, Sally ran to the pool, fumbled into her new suit and shot into the water before Mr. Busch could focus on her.

"I can see that new suit through the bubbles! Maybe I shouldn't let you out on weekends, after all," he laughed.

"Oh, no," she fibbed, "I'm not sacrificing my social life."

By not buying anything besides tooth-paste and shampoo, Sally saved enough for another swimsuit in three weeks. With Mr. Busch's words of admiration echoing in her mind, she bought another suit, and another, whenever she had enough money. The swimsuits piled up in her drawer, and whenever she looked at them, she felt good.

When some of the kids at school invited Sally to the amusement park, she refused, thinking first that she couldn't afford it, and second that they had taken too long before asking her to join them.

The day Sally dived past Mr. Busch in her fourth new suit, she glimpsed an attractive new girl standing beside him. As she swam back and forth, eyeing the newcomer, she noted with pleasure that her suit was more ragged than Sally's old one. The dye was streaked, there was a little hole at the waist, and it was so short for the girl that she tried to stretch it both up and down. Mr. Busch beckoned Sally out of the pool.

"This is Martina, a marvelous swimmer with no self-confidence. She's likely to think of how miserable she is in mid-stroke and sink to the bottom of the pool. The state meet is next month and I want you to work *together*," he emphasized, tapping Sally's nose.

Every day Sally measured Martina against herself. Martina's butterfly was stronger, her backstroke not as even. Sally could swim faster, but Martina could swim longer. Through the long hours of practice, Sally's initial resentment and jealously faded. Mutual respect and admiration grew between the two girls, but after practice, they always went their separate ways.

One afternoon, Martina shivered beside Mr. Busch, gripping his wrist while they timed Sally. Martina leaped to the edge of the pool, yelling, "You broke your own record. They can't beat you!"

When Martina began her endurance swimming, Sally shouted, "Go Raggedy Ann! One more hour and that old suit'll disintegrate." Sometimes Martina would retch, closing her eyes and swimming steadily until she recovered. Sally had never seen anyone swim beyond the point of discomfort and she knew that together they would win the meet, even though Martina started every practice saying, "I know I can't do it."

During the weekends, which seemed so long, Sally could hardly wait to rejoin Mr. Busch and Martina. She swam alone at the other pool until she almost fell asleep in the water. She purchased another suit and flung it into her drawer, noticing that she'd never taken the store tags off the last one.

Sunday she got to the pool early and did yoga exercises. When Mr. Busch and Martina arrived together, Martina's face was tear-stained, and she yanked at her suit more than usual.

"I was just telling Martina that you must have regulation suits for the state match," Mr. Busch said.

"I won't compete, then," interrupted Martina.

"How come?" asked Sally.

"I always wear this suit. I've had it for, for three years," she wailed.

"Well you certainly got your money's worth," joked Sally.

"It's not a life preserver," said Mr. Busch comfortingly.

"I can't swim without it, especially not at a meet," Martina shivered. "If I can't wear it I won't go!"

"That's ridiculous," laughed Sally, "You're such a good sw—"

Martina lunged toward Sally, shouting, "Don't call *me* ridiculous. *You're* ridiculous with your two hundred suits. It's a good thing they specified a suit for the meet or you'd spend the whole day trying to decide what to wear!"

Mr. Busch pulled Martina away, leaving Sally to practice alone. She's scared out of her mind, Sally thought.

When Sally got home that night, she scattered her bathing suits on the floor and counted them. She'd bought the first few with an excited feeling, the last ones out of habit.

Martina was right, she thought to herself. Ridiculous. Why did I buy them? What was all the scrimping and saving for, when I could have been having fun? I had my chance to make friends, but I blew it. And just to save for another stupid suit!

It suddenly seemed to her that she had been sick and recovered, and that these suits were the last symptoms of her illness. She went downstairs, calculating that her next check would arrive Wednesday.

"Hello, Martina," she said on the telephone. "I know the meet is coming right up, but we don't have to practice Friday night. Let's go to a movie, or whatever you want. My treat, OK?"

ACTIVITY 1 — Fact Questions

1. Where does Sally get her money?

2. Why did Sally's parents go back to Vermont?

3. Why did Sally's parents move to Florida in the first place?

4. How was Sally's life in Vermont different?

5. Did Sally really need the first new swimsuit she bought?

6. How did she save for the others?

7. Give two reasons why Sally refused to go to the amusement park.

8. What was Martina's problem?

9. What does Martina call Sally's habit of collecting swimsuits?

10. What does Sally ask Martina to do at the end of the story?

Copy this chart on your paper. Compute and record your WPM as you did on page 28.

Give yourself a score of 10 for each correct answer in Activity 1. This is your comprehension score. Record it on the chart.

	Hr.	Min.	Sec.
Ending time:	_____	_____	_____
Beginning time:	_____	_____	_____
Total Time:	_____	_____	_____

No. words:
No. seconds: $\left(\dfrac{1273}{}\right) \times 60 =$ _____ **WPM**

Comprehension Score: _____

ACTIVITY 2 — Thought Questions

1. Why does Mr. Busch want Sally to take off Friday and Saturday nights?

2. Why would Sally rather swim on weekends than go out with the other kids?

3. Why does she spend all her money on bathing suits?

4. Why do you think Mr. Busch's approval and admiration are so important to Sally?

5. Why did Sally note "with pleasure" that Martina's suit was ragged and too small?

6. What might be Mr. Busch's real reason for putting Sally and Martina together?

7. Why is the title of the story "Recovery"?

ACTIVITY 3 — Thinking About Conflict

1. What is Sally's conflict?

2. Does she attempt to resolve it directly or escape from it? Explain.

3. What does she *really* want? What does she replace it with?

4. Does buying the new suits solve the conflict?

5. How is the conflict finally resolved?

HOW TO READ IN SOCIAL STUDIES

In social studies, your understanding of the material you are reading often depends on how well you can follow and remember the sequence of events; that is, the order in which things happen. Knowing that one thing happened before or after another will help you increase your understanding of cause and effect as well as the outcomes of many problems and situations. History is the branch of social studies for which this skill is most important.

The article you are about to read gives the history of money as we know it today. As you read it, pay special attention to the order of events in the development of money.

Record your beginning and ending times.

Stacking gold at the Federal Reserve Bank of New York

What is a dollar really worth? What does it mean to you and to the person from whom you are buying something? What does it mean to the government? The following article will answer some of the questions you may have about money and what it means.

The History of Money _____

Written for this book
by Sheila Burns.

Several years ago in a major U.S. city, the government did not have enough money to pay its employees. "We'll pay them in scrip," said a city official. *Scrip* is a written promise to pay money at a later date.

"What? We won't take scrip. We must have real money," the employees said.

"Scrip and money are both the same," answered the city official. "They are both just pieces of paper."

The employees thought this over. Then they said, "But your scrip isn't worth anything. The government has gold in Fort Knox. We can always go to the bank and exchange our dollars for gold."

"You can't anymore," said the city official. "That's been changed. And even if you could, what would you do with gold? The grocery store won't take it. Neither will the gas station. Money is what we say it is. If we all say a piece of paper is money, then it's money."

Is that city official right? What is money anyway? How can just a piece of paper be valuable?

Many centuries ago, people had no need for money. They made most of what they wanted at home. If they needed something else, they traded for it. A person who had a lot of meat and no bread might exchange some extra meat for bread. Trading goods in this way is called *barter*.

But barter in large quantities was difficult because it was hard to carry trading goods around. A person who wanted to trade a herd of cattle could not move very quickly. In addition, the animals had to be guarded and cared for. Baskets of grain were heavy to carry. So were jars of oil and bundles of cloth.

To make barter easier, people set up regular times and places for trading. On certain days they met at a crossroads or a large open space. In this way, market-places began.

But even with the help of markets, people still had difficulty finding the right thing at the right time. To get what they wanted, people had to make several trades. A farmer who arrived at market with a load of wheat might trade wheat for cattle. Later, perhaps the next week, the same farmer might need some cloth. Then he could trade some of the cattle for the cloth.

Soon people measured their possessions by what they were worth in trade. A fast horse might be worth three cows. A necklace could be worth ten cows. In this way cattle became a form of money in some places.

Other people used different things for money. In cold climates they used furs. Hunters or fighters used spearheads. And some people used shells, feathers, and even teeth.

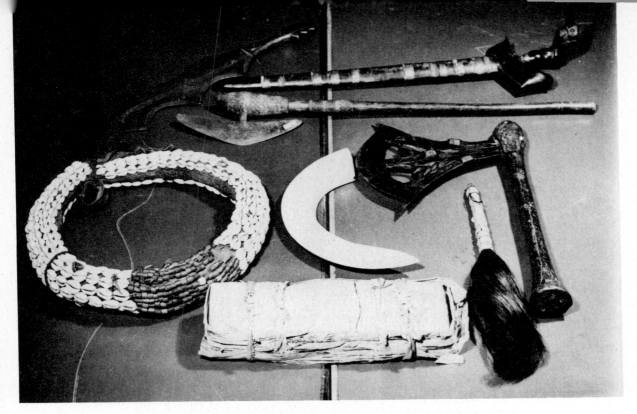

Objects once used as money in various parts of the world

Around the Mediterranean Sea metal was used as money. People discovered that iron hammers and axes worked better than stone ones. Copper pots lasted longer than clay. As a result, metal objects became valuable.

Soon measured weights of certain metals were used to pay debts. Greeks made a copper nail which was worth one ox. Other people molded gold and silver into bars which they then used as money.

As soon as metal bars were used for money, people thought of a way to cheat. To the bars they added low-grade metal. Once someone even made a bar of mud and coated it with gold.

Merchants needed a way to protect themselves from being cheated. The merchants molded and weighed lumps of metal themselves. They stamped the bars with their seals. Then they could be sure that the stamped pieces of metal were good.

Soon the king of that country decided that he should stamp the money instead of letting the merchants do it. He put his own seal onto coins, which were carried by traders throughout the Mediterranean. Using metal pieces as money was such a good idea that other rulers made coins of their own.

In time, people replaced metal money with paper. Rather than keep their gold and silver at home, merchants left their coins with a local goldsmith who was able to guard them. In return for the coins, each person was given a note called a receipt. The receipt said that the merchant had deposited the gold or silver with the goldsmith. When the merchants did business, they could use these receipts instead of coins. They found it easier and safer to use paper in place of metal.

In this way, paper came to be used as money. Soon governments controlled the production of that paper. And because people have faith in their government, they have faith in the value of money issued by that government.

The value of money may also depend on the amount produced by the people who use it. Many people who study the theory of money say that money is only a way to measure the amount of work that has been poured into a product.

If this is so, then it may be true that money *is* only what we say it is. In fact, no one is very sure that he or she fully understands money. And the more we think about it, the more complicated it seems.

ACTIVITY 1

Putting Events in Sequence

Here are several events in the development of money. Number your paper from 1 to 5. Write the letter of each event on your paper in the order in which it occurred.

a. Metal money was replaced with paper.

b. Metal bars were used for money.

c. Kings put their seals on coins.

d. Measured weights of metals were used to pay debts.

e. Furs, shells, and other objects were used for money.

ACTIVITY 2

Thinking About Money

Here is a list of things that have been used for money. Following the list are five qualities that money must have. On your paper write the letter of the quality or qualities that each numbered item lacks.

In other words, tell why each is *not* a good form of money.

1. cows
2. bundles of wheat
3. shells
4. jars of wine
5. metal nails

a. Each unit is the same as every other unit of the same value.

b. It must be available in smaller and larger units to show differences in value.

c. It must be able to be saved for long periods of time without spoiling, breaking, or losing value.

d. It should be easy to identify so it can't be copied.

e. It should be easy to move or carry from place to place.

Copy this chart on your paper. Compute and record your WPM as you did on page 28.

Give yourself a score of 10 for each correct answer in Activity 1 and Activity 2. This is your comprehension score. Record it on the chart.

	Hr.	Min.	Sec.
Ending time:	_____	_____	_____
Beginning time:	_____	_____	_____
Total Time:	_____	_____	_____
No. words: No. seconds:	$\left(\dfrac{865}{}\right) \times 60 =$ _____ **WPM**		

Comprehension Score: _____

Many science articles are written for the purpose of helping people improve their everyday lives. They may deal with health, child care, the environment, and other topics. In order to get the most out of such articles, you must read them carefully. Even more, you must learn to remember the information they contain and try to use it whenever you can.

The following science article can be helpful to you in learning to spend your money more wisely. Read it carefully and try to remember the important information it contains.

How far can you make a dollar go? How carefully do you think before you buy something? Do you compare what you are buying with other similar products? After reading the next article, your habits in these areas may change a little.

Be a Better Buyer

Written for this book by Leonard Bernstein.

You became a consumer the first time you bought something in a store. It may have been only a piece of gum, and suddenly you became a member of a club. You joined the group of millions of American consumers.

Almost anyone can be a consumer—all you need is the cash. The point is to become a wise consumer. The way to do that is to spend money wisely. Do you know what you want to buy and how much it should cost? Do you shop around and compare prices before you buy? And what about the laws that protect you as a consumer? Do you know them? If your answer to all of these questions is no, don't

feel too bad—you're not alone. Many members of the club are in the same boat as you. But let's check it out; not at the counter, right here! Here's what being a wise consumer means.

The value of the dollar is going down and the price of almost everything is going up. One thing you can do about it is to learn how to shop. Here are examples of some of the things you should be looking for.

Case I: It's All American

Imagine two packages of cheese, each having the same weight, each containing

158

16 slices, each made by the same company. In one package, all the slices are individually wrapped. It costs $1.19. In the other package, the slices are not individually wrapped. It's not so neat, but just as tasty and healthful. It costs $1.09. The consumer (you?) pays 10 cents for wrapping and doesn't even eat the paper!

Case II: Bubbles Burn a Hole in Your Pocket

Almost everyone likes soda. But look at the variety: 6-ounce bottles, 8-ounce bottles, one-liter bottles, cans, 6-packs, 8-packs. With all the different sizes, price can certainly become confusing. Which is the best buy? How do you find out? Do you take out your pencil and pad? Do you whip out your trusty pocket calculator? Do you dash to the nearest phone and call your favorite math teacher and quietly scream for help? Don't panic! Don't make a scene. Just look for the words *unit price*. The unit price for soda is the price per ounce or quart. It's printed somewhere. Look for it! The least expensive unit price could be the best buy. At least it lets you make a fair comparison.

Case III: Is What You See What You Get?

Foods come in a variety of packages. Packaging serves many purposes. One of these is to make the food look attractive. (As a matter of fact, very often the picture looks better than the food in the package.)

There are many things you should look for when buying packaged foods. Read the label carefully. Is everything you think is in the package really there? Compare brands. Check and compare price against weight. Watch out for packages that are torn or broken. Don't buy a can of food if the can is badly dented. Dented cans may have a broken seal and the food may be spoiled or poisoned. Another important thing to look for is the date of expiration. Certain foods should not be sold after that date. In addition, foods with a later date of expiration will be fresher and will last longer. Don't be ashamed to do these things, after all, it's your money you're spending.

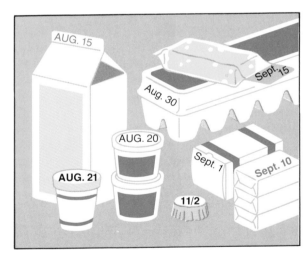

Case IV: The Consumer at Home

You can be a wise consumer at home too. This means using energy wisely, especially electrical energy. The electric company in your town or city can give you information about using electrical appliances

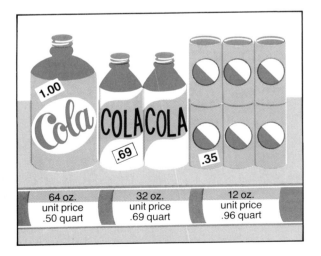

| 64 oz. unit price .50 quart | 32 oz. unit price .69 quart | 12 oz. unit price .96 quart |

wisely. It can also tell you how much it costs to operate these appliances. Now the unit price becomes the *kilowatt hour*. Using the price per kilowatt hour, you can learn how much it costs to operate a TV, hairdryer, toaster, radio, and many other electrical appliances. Some of these costs might surprise you. They might also help you decide which electrical appliances to buy, as well as how to use them. Finally, you might really believe that it does pay to turn off that light when you leave a room.

ACTIVITY 1
How Carefully Did You Read?

1. Why are individually wrapped cheese slices more expensive than bulk-packaged cheese?

2. Why is it unwise to buy dented cans?

3. How can pictures on packages be misleading?

4. Why should you buy foods with the latest expiration dates?

5. What is the unit price related to when measuring the cost of electricity?

ACTIVITY 2
Being a Good Consumer

How good a consumer are you at home? Think about each of the situations described below. On your paper, describe what a wise household consumer would do in each situation and why.

1. The shirt that you want to wear to the game tomorrow is dirty, but there are not enough other clothes to make a full load in the machine.

2. You are alone in the living room, watching television. You go to your room to study, but you think you will come back to watch another program after you finish.

3. You and your brother both have to go in the same direction to do errands on Saturday morning. He suggests that you let him take the car first, and you use it later.

4. The thermostat in your house is set for 70°, and your family is going away for the weekend. You want the house to be warm when you get back.

HOW TO READ IN MATHEMATICS

One of the many practical ways to use mathematics is in solving problems concerning money. You need to solve problems of this type when you compare prices in the supermarket, or figure out how much it costs each time you run your washing machine. Good consumers need mathematics skills to figure out exactly how much they are spending for what they are getting.

The terms used in money problems can be confusing, because monetary values are expressed in so many different ways. For example, the same amount may be written out in words (ten cents, or a dime), in numbers with signs (10¢), or in decimals ($.10). You need to know how to read, and understand at a glance, money values when expressed in different ways. For problem solving, it is most important to develop skill in reading decimals.

You will have to concentrate hard when you read the following article, because you will find terms expressing British as well as United States money values.

Following the Revolutionary War, the system of money used by merchants and shipowners in the Colonies was very confusing. Coins of England, Portugal, and the United States were exchanged freely. English pence, shillings, and pounds, as well as American dollars, were quite common. When Jefferson became President, he found a solution to this confusing situation. In this article, you will find out about the system he introduced.

Money Values After the Revolutionary War _____

Written for this book
by William L. Schaaf.

The English units used for money values at the time of the Continental Congresses were rather awkward:

> 12 pence (12d.) = 1 shilling (1s.)
> 20 shillings = 1 pound (£1).
> 21 shillings = 1 guinea (1g.)

To make matters even worse, American dollars did not have the same value in all the Colonies. Thus, a dollar was worth 8 shillings in New York, but only 4 shillings 8 pence in South Carolina.

The Continental Congresses did several important things. One of them was to establish the decimal system of money which we still use today:

> 10 cents = 1 dime
> 10 dimes = 1 dollar

You know that Thomas Jefferson wrote

the Declaration of Independence. It was also through his efforts that our present system of money was introduced. This system is based upon powers of ten; that is why we call it a *decimal system*. (The word *decimal* means *counted by tens*.) Actually, it is just like our system for writing numbers.

For example, 348 means:

$$348 = 300 + 40 + 8$$
$$= 3(100) + 4(10) + 8(1)$$
$$= 3(10)^2 + 4(10)^1 + 8(10)^0$$

Similarly, the sum of money $3.48 means:

$$348 \text{ cents} = 300¢ + 40¢ + 8¢$$
$$= 3(100¢) + 4(10¢) + 8(1¢)$$
$$= 3 \text{ dollars} + 4 \text{ dimes} + 8 \text{ cents}$$

Indeed, Jefferson regarded the *dime* as a separate unit, like the *cent* and the *dollar*. In those days the abbreviation for *dollar* was D. Thus he wrote 2.75D instead of $2.75, and for him it meant "2 dollars + 7 dimes + 5 cents." He also wrote 8.5D instead of $8.50, which shows that he thought of half a dollar as 5 *dimes* rather than as 50 *cents*: thus 8.5D meant to him 8 dollars + 5 dimes.

Answer the following questions on your paper.

1. How many cents are there in one dollar?

2. What fractional part of a dollar is one cent?

3. How many dimes are there in a dollar?

4. What fractional part of a dollar is one dime?

On your paper, write each of these amounts using a dollar sign ($).

For example, 15¢ = $.15.
1. 12 cents
2. 16¢
3. 5¢
4. 40¢
5. a quarter
6. 75 cents
7. a dime

On your paper, write each of these sums of money using a dollar sign and numbers.

For example, two dollars and seventy-five cents = $2.75.

1. six dollars and seven cents
2. nine dollars and thirty-eight cents
3. nine cents
4. ninety cents
5. ten dollars

163

Making Comparisons and Contrasts

One of the skills which you need to use most often in geography, history, or social studies is making comparisons and contrasts. This skill is often necessary in studying science and mathematics, too. In making comparisons you study two countries, two classes of plants or animals, two numbers or sets of numbers, or other topics to find how they are alike. In making contrasts, you find out how they are different. Sometimes you examine two topics for the purpose of both comparing and contrasting.

Read each of the following selections. As you read the one on Greenland, think of the ways in which this country is like Iceland and the ways in which it is different from Iceland.

Iceland

A main street in Reykjavik

Iceland is an island in the North Atlantic Ocean. It is about midway between Norway and Greenland. Its northerly part touches the Arctic Circle, but the entire island lies below the Arctic Circle. The area of the island is 39,768 square miles (98,397 square kilometers).

The largest part of Iceland is a high plateau. This plateau is covered with glaciers, snowfields, or rock. No part of this plateau is of any use for growing crops or for anything else. All the people in Iceland live on the lower lands along the shores of the sea.

A warm current of the Gulf Stream usually encircles the island. This makes the climate much milder than it might otherwise be. The capital, Reykjavik, has an average temperature in January of 39.4° F (4° C). The average temperature in July is 51.6° F (10.8° C).

Several kinds of mosses grow in Iceland. The most famous of these mosses is called *Iceland moss*. This moss is dried and used for making bread, or is eaten with milk. Heather covers large parts of Iceland and is used for pasture for sheep. There is little in Iceland in the way of forest trees. There are a few birches, a few mountain ash, and some willows here and there. But forests as such are not found in Iceland.

Reykjavik (rāk′yə vēk), the capital of Iceland.

Greenland

Greenland is an island lying in the North Atlantic Ocean above the north-eastern part of the United States. It is the largest island in the world. It has an area of 827,275 square miles (2,150,915 square kilometers). The greater part of this island lies above the Arctic Circle.

A great icecap covers the entire central part of Greenland. The area of this icecap is about 721,000 square miles (1,874,600 square kilometers). So you see, there is not too much space left where people can live. The only part that is inhabited is the land along the coast.

Since the island is so far north, the climate is very cold. The average temperature in January ranges from −30° F (−34.4° C) in the north to 20° F (−6.7° C) in the south. In July the average is 40° F (4.4° C). The warm Gulf Stream causes the temperature to be warmest in the southwest of Greenland, on the coast.

In some parts of Greenland the ground is covered with a carpet of mosses. There are no forests on this island. There are a few dwarf birch trees and willows here and there. Some vegetables grow in the south, but farms as such do not exist.

Activity 1

Each of the paragraphs in the articles on Iceland and Greenland deals with a different topic. The topic of the first paragraph in each article is "Location and Area." Write the ways in which Iceland and Greenland are alike in location and area. Then write the ways in which the two countries are different in location and area.

In the same way, write the likenesses and differences for each of the other three topics listed. Use your own paper.

1. Location and Area
2. Surface
3. Climate
4. Vegetation

Another view of Reykjavik

Critical Reading: What Labels Tell You

Do you always have maple syrup on your pancakes? Maybe you do, but more likely you only think that's what you're having. The syrups most people pour over their pancakes and waffles may contain less than 3 percent real maple syrup—or none at all. The labels on the popular brands of pancake syrups do not even call the contents maple syrup; but most customers are surprised to learn that most of what they are getting is sugar or corn syrup, artificial coloring and flavoring, and preservatives.

Intelligent consumers should consider the ingredients of the canned and packaged foods they buy, as well as price and advertising claims. Manufacturers are required to list the ingredients of their products on the labels, but too often the labels remain unread or are not understood. If you want to know what goes into what you are buying and using, you should get into the habit of reading the list of ingredients.

Read each of the following lists of ingredients in common products and, on your paper, write the answers to the questions that follow.

A. A low-calorie soft drink:

"Carbonated water, citric acid, sodium saccharin [7.3 mg. (less than 0.03%) saccharin per fluid oz., a non-nutritive artificial sweetener which should be used only by persons who must restrict their intake of ordinary sweets], 0.03% sodium benzoate as a preservative, sodium citrate, and natural lemon and lime flavors."

1. What is the main ingredient in this soft drink?
2. How can you be sure whether you are one of the people who "must restrict their intake of ordinary sweets"?
3. Is the flavoring natural or artificial?

B. Brand Y Bread:

"Enriched flour, water, corn sweeteners, shortening, yeast, salt, dough conditioners, yeast nutrients, calcium propionate (added to retard spoilage)."

Brand Z Bread:

"Unbleached flour, water, corn syrup, liquid vegetable shortening (soy bean and cottonseed), fresh yeast, salt, honey, U.S. Grade AA sweet creamery butter, dough conditioner."

1. Which brand uses butter?
2. Which brand seems to contain more natural ingredients?
3. Which one contains a chemical preservative?

MUST YOU READ EVERY WORD ON EVERY SINGLE LABEL?

Working with Social Studies Words

The words below are used frequently in social studies and history textbooks. It will be helpful to you to know the pronunciation and meaning of each of these words.

Work out the pronunciation of each word. Say the word distinctly. Study the meaning of the word and think about it.

---

aggression (ə gresh′ən), act of hostility; an unprovoked attack.

alienate (āl′yən āt), to turn away in feeling and affection, make unfriendly.

competition (kom′pə tish′ən), a struggle or contest between two people or groups of people to see which one is better at something.

coordinate (kō ôr′də nāt), to combine things, activities, or people together in good relationships.

corporation (kôr′pə rā shən), a group of persons organized by law to carry on a business or a particular kind of work and to act as one person.

expertise (ek spẽr tēz′), expertness in skills, knowledge; know-how.

ghetto (get′ō), any part of a city inhabited largely by one minority group; usually a thickly populated section.

negotiation (ni gō′shē ā′shən), talking over and arranging terms.

retaliate (ri tal′ē āt), to pay back a harmful action with a similar action; to get revenge.

society (sə sī′ə tē), all people; the people and customs that are associated with a particular time and place.

See if you know the meaning of each of these words as it is used in social studies. On your paper, write the word that belongs in each blank space. Add *s* or *d* if necessary.

1. The colonists tried to _____ when the British attacked them.

2. King George III _____ many colonists when he refused to consider their appeals.

3. Most schools have baseball teams that enter into _____ with the teams of other schools.

4. The captain tried to _____ the activities of the lieutenants under his command.

5. The heads of two governments that were at war tried to settle the war by means of peaceful talks and _____.

6. If one country starts a war to conquer another one, it is committing an act of _____.

7. Cities are trying to improve living conditions in _____ where people are crowded together.

8. A group of men interested in selling real estate formed a _____ to carry on their business.

9. Some United States space scientists offered to share their _____ with a group of people who wanted to hear about our latest spaceflights.

10. As a member of modern American _____, you are part of the people and customs of this country at the present time.

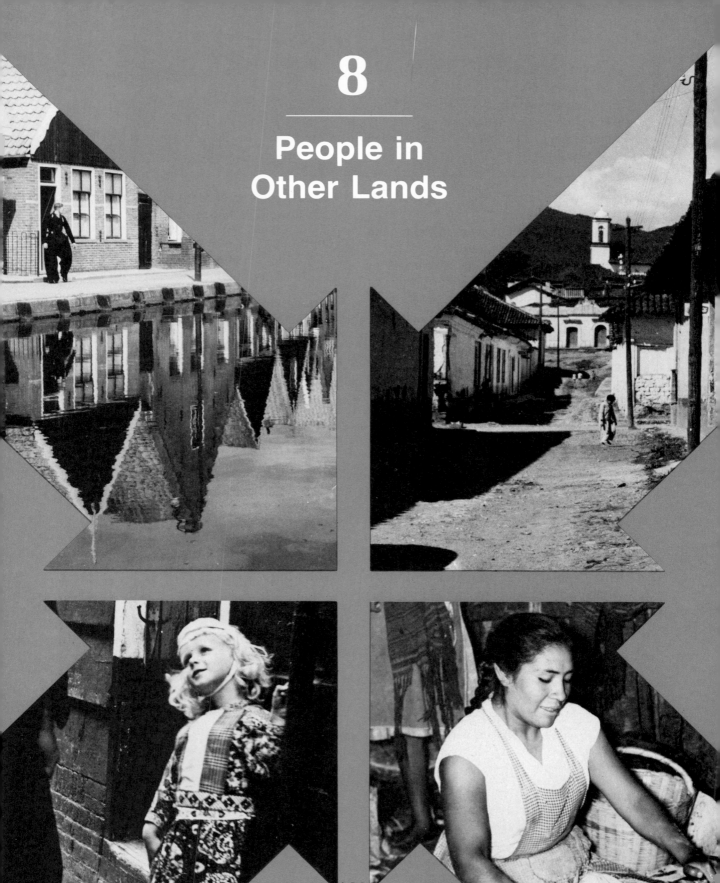

8

People in
Other Lands

168

HOW TO READ LITERATURE

Earlier you read that the theme is the main idea or meaning of the story. In some kinds of stories, the author may put the theme into words at some point in the story. In other stories, you have to figure out the theme for yourself. An author may give you hints about the theme in things the characters think, feel, or say, or in the way the conflict is resolved. Often the title an author chooses for a story is a clue to the theme.

As you read the story "The Lion's Eye," think about what the theme might be—or what the story means. When you have finished the story, you should be able to give the theme in a sentence or two.

Record your beginning and ending times.

Many young people are often critical of the way their parents and other older people live. In the next story, you will read about a young African girl who feels this way, and you will see how she resolves her conflict.

The Lion's Eye

Written for this book
by Juliana O. Muehrcke.

"Aren't you packed yet?" asked Safini. "The bus is coming this afternoon."

"I'm not going home," Tama said.

Tama saw her friend's eyes widen in surprise. "Not going home! But *everyone's* going home for vacation."

Tama wiggled uncomfortably. How could she explain?

The two girls were sitting in the shade of a mango tree outside their school. Thorny bushes and savanna grass grew right up to the school gate. On the distant slopes, Tama could see wild antelope grazing.

Tama loved her school, set in the midst of the rolling plains of Uganda, Africa. Yet now she was worried. She *couldn't* go home to her village for vacation. But would Safini understand?

Luckily, Tama didn't have to answer. A group of girls came up, calling to Safini. They spoke in Swahili, the widely known language that helped the many different tribes in Africa understand one another.

You'd never know, Tama thought, that these girls all belonged to different tribes and spoke different languages at home. In the old days, tribal marks would have been cut into their faces. Thank goodness that was rarely done nowadays!

But many of the old African ways still hung on. That's what bothered Tama. Here at school she had learned modern ways. How could she go back to the ignorance and superstition of her village?

Tama jumped up. She broke away from the girls in the mango grove and dashed off across the plains. She didn't want to answer any questions about why she wasn't going home.

But when she slowed to a walk, she heard the rustle of grass behind her. It was Safini.

"Now," said Safini, falling into step beside Tama, "why aren't you going home? What will your father say?"

"He'll be angry," Tama said, "but I don't care!" All her stored-up feelings came pouring out. "He expects me to do everything in the old way, and I won't! At school I've learned new, better ways of doing things."

"Have you told your father that?" Safini asked.

"No, what good would it do? He still believes in magic and medicine men!"

"So does my father," said Safini. "When someone is sick, he does the old dances to drive out the evil spirits."

---

mango (maŋ′gō), a yellow-red juicy fruit.

savanna grass (sə van′ə gras), grass growing on the plains.

acacia (ə kā′shə), a tree or shrub of the mimosa family.

170

"How can you reason with someone like that?" Tama demanded. "Why, Father still believes that men are superior to women!"

"I know," said Safini. "A proper village woman must bow down to men and always serve the men first. Men use forks and spoons, but women eat with their hands. Old customs like that are hard to change."

"Well, I've learned that women are equal to men," Tama said. "I *won't* be treated as an inferior! And I won't let my father decide whom I will marry. *I'll* decide. Maybe I won't get married at all. Today a girl can plan her own life."

"Surely your father would understand how you feel if you just explain to him."

"Never!" Tama's cry was from her heart.

"Change comes slowly," Safini admitted. "It's hard to give up things you've believed for hundreds of rains."

"Yes," Tama said bitterly. "Hundreds of rains." In Uganda there were only two seasons—the rainy and the dry season, and time was measured in rains rather than years.

"I won't be part of the old ways!" Tama insisted. "I don't *belong* in the village, and I won't go back!"

Thoughtfully, Safini munched on a juicy yellow mango. "People like us," she said, "are the link between the new Africa and the old. It's up to us to bring the two together. We must explain the new ways to our parents. But we mustn't turn our backs on the old ways."

"My father will never listen to me!" Tama cried.

"Perhaps not at first. But give him time. All over Africa, people *are* beginning to listen."

Without answering, Tama walked on through a grove of tall flat-topped acacia

trees. She was so full of anger she didn't notice the strange, unnatural silence that fell over the plains.

Suddenly Safini gave a gasp. *"Simba!"* she breathed in sharp warning.

Simba was the Swahili word for lion. Tama stopped dead. And then she saw it.

The lion was just ahead. Its tawny shape blended into the tall yellow grass as if it were a part of it. It stood perfectly still, its huge head held high and proud.

Tama's heart beat faster. But she wasn't afraid. As a child, she had learned not to fear wild animals. She knew they rarely attacked except for food or to defend themselves.

For a long moment Tama stared into the calm golden eyes of the lion, and those eyes spoke to her. They spoke of courage and beauty and freedom.

Tama's heart soared. Only an African, she thought, could know this special link between humans and beasts. Most of the old customs were based on this deep feeling of the African for the animals that shared the land.

The lion turned without a sound. It dissolved into the golden savanna grass and disappeared.

But Tama remembered those yellow eyes. For centuries, she thought, Africans had watched the animals and learned things from them that couldn't be found in schoolbooks. Tama felt a rush of pride for the African people, living in close union with the wilderness around them.

Yes, Tama thought, there was beauty and bravery in the old ways. There was much that was worth saving. Just as there was good—and bad—in the new ways. If the good in both new and old were combined, how great Africa could be!

She would tell her father that. Suddenly she was sure he would understand.

"Let's hurry back," Tama said. "I have to pack. I don't want to miss the bus for home!"

ACTIVITY 1 — Fact Questions

1. Who was Safini?

2. What type of landscape was there around Tama's school?

3. Where was the school?

4. How do the different African tribes understand each other?

5. In the old days, how could you tell at a glance what tribe an African person belonged to?

6. Why didn't Tama want to go home?

7. What doesn't she like about the old ways?

8. What two seasons are there in Uganda?

9. Why wasn't Tama afraid of the lion?

10. Why was Tama proud of the African people?

Copy this chart on your paper. Compute and record your WPM as you did on page 28.

Give yourself a score of 10 for each correct answer in Activity 1. This is your comprehension score. Record it on the chart.

	Hr.	Min.	Sec.
Ending time:	___	___	___
Beginning time:	___	___	___
Total Time:	___	___	___

No. words: No. seconds: $\left(\dfrac{953}{}\right) \times 60 = $ ___ **WPM**

Comprehension Score: ___

ACTIVITY 2 — Thought Questions

1. Why did Tama think her father wouldn't listen to her?

2. Why did Safini think she and Tama were the link between old and new Africa?

3. What did the lion's eyes tell Tama?

4. What decision did Tama make after seeing the lion?

ACTIVITY 3 — Thinking About Theme

1. Give the theme of the story in a sentence or two.

2. What things that the characters say, think, or feel before the end help you know what the theme is?

3. Find the place in the story where the author makes the theme clear.

1. In reading this social studies selection, first glance quickly through the entire selection to find the topic or subject of each paragraph. The topic is different from the main idea. The topic is the subject or theme that each paragraph discusses. Think of the topic as a title of the paragraph. Write this title in a few words on your paper. Write titles only for the numbered paragraphs.

2. After finding and writing the topic or subject of each paragraph, reread the selection carefully to find out all the details about each topic. Listing the details about each topic is a good way to make comparisons later. You will be asked to compare the lives of Camilo and Irene.

In the story you just read, you learned something about the life of a girl in modern Africa. Read the next article to learn about the lives of people in two other countries.

Alike, Yet Different _____

Written for this book
by John Heine.

Camilo

Camilo is a 14-year-old Mexican Indian boy who lives on a small island in Lake Patzcuaro. Lake Patzcuaro is about 150 miles (240 kilometers) west of Mexico City, the capital of Mexico.

Camilo (kə mē′lō), a Spanish name for a boy.

Patzcuaro (patz kwä′rō), the name of a lake in the southern part of Mexico.

adobe (ə dō′bē), clay or mud that is sun-dried.

tortilla (tôr tē′yə), a thin, flat, round corncake.

chile pepper (chil′ē pep′ĕr), a very hot-tasting kind of red or green vegetable.

fiesta (fē es′tə), a religious holiday.

Netherlands (neth′ĕr ləndz), a small country in western Europe, sometimes called *Holland* (hol′ənd).

Edam (ē′dam), a kind of cheese made by the Dutch.

1. Camilo's home is a one-room house built of adobe bricks. At night he sleeps on a woven mat spread on the floor. He covers himself with a bright blanket called a serape. On one side of the room is a beehive-shaped oven used by Camilo's mother and sisters for baking. Jugs on a shelf are used for storing water. On one wall hang copper kettles, cooking pots, and brightly painted pottery. A wooden chest is used for storing clothing. Several fishing nets are usually hung to dry at one side of the room.

2. At almost every meal, Camilo's family eats tortillas. These are thin corncakes baked by his mother or sisters. With the tortillas, Camilo usually has kidney

beans and fish taken from the lake. The usual drink is a thin soup made from corn. The food is often spiced with chile peppers. Sometimes Camilo has onions, tomatoes, garlic, squash, sweet potatoes, or fresh fruit. Since meat is expensive, Camilo's family is able to buy meat only for special days and holidays.

3. Camilo looks forward eagerly to fiestas. These are usually religious holidays, including saints' days. He and other children in his village dress up and wear masks. The fiesta often has a parade, followed by dances in which groups of children take part. At one of the fiestas, a contest is held in which men and boys try to ride a bull by holding onto it with only a strap.

Irene

Irene's life is different from Camilo's in many ways. She lives in northern Holland or the Netherlands. Irene goes to school, for the law requires that everyone between the ages of 7 and 14 must attend school. Her favorite subject is English, which she has been studying for several years.

1. Irene's home is built of brick, with a steeply sloping tile roof and brightly painted shutters. Most of the houses in the Netherlands are built of brick, tile, or concrete rather than wood, because most of the wood used in the Netherlands must be imported. The furniture in Irene's home is simple and somewhat old-fashioned compared to that in American homes.

2. Irene's parents pride themselves on setting a good table. Many meals include dishes using the famous Edam cheese, which her father makes. Bread, butter, meat, potatoes, and fresh milk are usually served, also. Irene's family

has a vegetable garden which helps keep them supplied. She is fond of herring and other fish, which her mother buys at the weekly market in a nearby town. Irene often helps her mother bake cookies or make preserves that are served as dessert.

3. Like most Netherlanders, Irene enjoys riding her bicycle along the brick roads near her home. Few people own automobiles, so the bicycle is the most common form of transportation in Irene's country. When the weather is cold, Irene likes to go on skating parties on one of the many nearby canals. In summer she often goes swimming at a beach a few miles from her home. Sometimes Irene goes to watch her brother play his favorite game, soccer, with the boys from his school.

1 ACTIVITY

Making Comparisons

On your paper, make a chart like this one. Fill in the topic you wrote for each paragraph. Under each topic, write three details mentioned in the paragraph. When you have finished, you will find that you have made a comparison of the lives of Camilo and Irene.

Camilo	Irene
1. Camilo's Home Details: **a.** **b.** **c.**	1. _____ Details: **a.** **b.** **c.**

**HOW TO READ IN
SCIENCE**

In science, it is very important to pay careful attention to details. Sometimes, a harmless chemical, plant, or creature is only slightly different from one that is deadly. Comparing and contrasting details is a good way of identifying things.

As you read the science article that follows, use the skills of comparison and contrast to tell the difference between the various kinds of fish discussed.

Record your beginning and ending times.

All over the world, swimmers and bathers share one great fear. Read the following article to learn more about what they fear and why.

Shark! _____

Written for this book
by Leonard Bernstein.

Fear is something that almost everyone has experienced at one time or another. Sometimes the fear is imagined; sometimes it is very real. People fear the unknown, the mysterious. Even a word can be a symbol of terror and danger. Just hearing the word can be terrifying.

Imagine the seashore on a hot summer day. The waves gently roll in toward the shore. You splash in and start swimming out. It's cool and refreshing. You glance around and the beach is not too far away. You know you can reach it in less than a minute; you've done it so many times before. Suddenly, the air is shattered by a scream. You hear only one word. *Shark!*

Much has been written about sharks, but very little is really known about them. Even identifying a shark in the water can be very difficult.

The back, or dorsal, fin of a shark is one of its clearest characteristics. However, it may easily be confused with the fin or wing tip of other sea animals that do not usually harm people. The porpoise, a small whale, has a dorsal fin, but shows a part of its back as it moves in the water. The swordfish also has a dorsal fin, but in addition it displays a portion of its tail. The manta ray, or giant devilfish, looks terrifying, but it is known to be harmless. As it moves, each of its wing tips may break the surface and give the appearance of sharks swimming side by side.

Sharks are among the earth's oldest groups of animals. Some types are known to have survived almost unchanged for as long as 250 million years. Their ability for survival, strength, and speed—and their appetite—is almost unequaled in the entire animal world. A shark's teeth are arranged in rows and can number as many as 280 in the tiger shark to more than 1,500 in the whale shark. Sharks' teeth are the largest in the fish world. Some are grinding teeth, like our molars, some are pointed, and some have jagged edges.

Most sharks are found in tropical and temperate seas where the water temperature is fairly warm. However, sharks can be found at nearly all latitudes on earth. There is even a species that makes its home in the frigid waters of the Arctic, the Greenland shark.

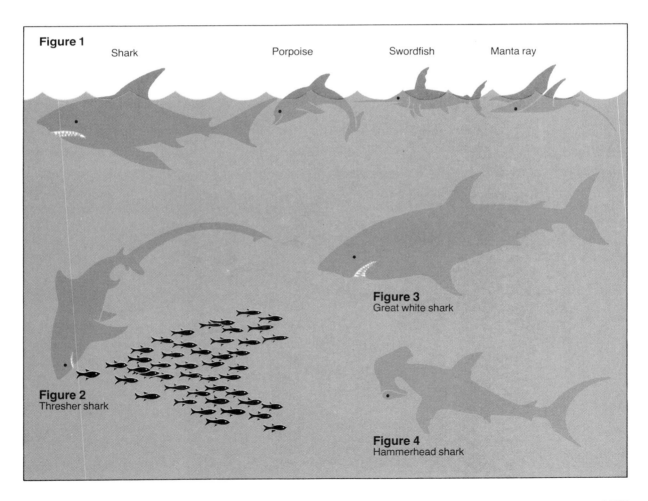

Figure 1
Shark   Porpoise   Swordfish   Manta ray

Figure 2
Thresher shark

Figure 3
Great white shark

Figure 4
Hammerhead shark

The shark is not limited to the oceans and seas. Many have been known to move up rivers in search of food. In India, sharks have attacked people in river waters 100 miles (160 kilometers) from the open sea. Another species, called the bull shark, has established a home in the fresh water of Lake Nicaragua in Central America. This variety of shark grows to a length of about 10 feet (3 meters). It has two rows of razor-sharp teeth. Bull sharks have attacked people as they were swimming in Lake Nicaragua.

The hunting and feeding patterns of sharks are of great interest to oceanographers. They have been known to eat sea turtles, birds, fish, lobsters, crabs, garbage, large and small animals, clothing, tin cans, and, in the case of some species, even people. The bite is an unmistakable crescent shape. It is often so deep that major blood vessels are cut and death follows quickly.

The thresher shark is an eager and skilled hunter. It has an unusually long tail. This shark circles a school of fish and uses its tail to beat them into a crowded mass. Then the thresher shark moves through the mass and feeds on the fish.

The most dangerous shark is the great white shark, also called the white death. Great white sharks may grow to a length of 25 feet (7.6 meters). They have been known to attack human beings and even small boats for no apparent reason. They are powerful swimmers and are feared by fishing crews who work in tropical waters.

A close second to the great white shark is the tiger shark. The mouth of the tiger shark is filled with five or six rows of teeth. The bite of this fish is so powerful that it can cut through the shell of a large sea turtle. Tiger sharks are considered to be the most dangerous sharks in India, South Africa, Australia, and the Philippines. Like the great white shark, they have been known to smash into boats and knock people overboard.

Other kinds of sharks that have attacked people are the mako, the hammerhead, and the blue shark. These sharks are among the 25 species that have been known to attack human beings. Evidently, there is good reason for the warning: "Leave the water immediately if a shark is sighted."

ACTIVITY 1

Write the answers to these questions on your own paper.

1. Why is it difficult to identify a shark in the water?

2. How are a shark's teeth arranged?

3. Describe the teeth of sharks.

4. How do we know that sharks are not limited to living in the oceans and seas?

5. What kinds of things do sharks eat?

6. Describe the shape of a shark bite and explain why it is so dangerous.

7. What is an unusual feature and feeding pattern of the thresher shark?

8. Why is the great white shark called the white death?

9. About how many species of sharks are known to be dangerous to human beings?

10. What should you do if you are swimming and a shark is sighted?

Copy this chart on your paper. Compute and record your WPM as you did on page 28.

Give yourself a score of 10 for each correct answer in Activity 1. This is your comprehension score. Record it on the chart.

	Hr.	Min.	Sec.
Ending time:	——	——	——
Beginning time:	——	——	——
Total Time:	——	——	——

No. words:
No. seconds: $\left(\dfrac{783}{\quad}\right) \times 60 =$ ——— **WPM**

Comprehension Score: ———

ACTIVITY 2

Comparison and Contrast

Look at Figure 1, and reread the fourth paragraph of "Shark!" On your own paper, make a chart like this one and fill in the similarities and differences.

	Similarities	Differences
Shark		
Porpoise		
Swordfish		
Manta ray		

WHEW! I THOUGHT YOU WERE A SHARK.

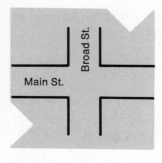

HOW TO READ IN MATHEMATICS

In this lesson you will learn how mathematicians describe and measure distances between points. Here, as in your other mathematics lessons in this book, you will need to read several different kinds of symbols: letters, diagrams, words, and numerals. You will need to understand special mathematical terms, such as *perpendicular, segment, bisect, intersection,* and *radius.* You will also have a chance to work some problems similar to some you may have to solve in real life. See how well you can read this mathematics lesson, which is quite different from the other selections in this unit.

In this unit you have read about people in other lands— Africa, Mexico, and the Netherlands. Suppose you were to travel to one of these countries. How far would you travel? How would you find the airline distance or the number of miles between your home and a distant point? How would you compare the distances between different points?

Distances Between Points _____

Written for this book
by William L. Schaaf.

The "airline" distance between two cities means the distance in a straight line, rather than the twists and turns of railroads and highways.

We speak of a line as passing through two points, such as A and B.

---

perpendicular (pĕr′pən dik′ū lĕr), at right angles, as a floor and a wall; a line at right angles.

bisector (bī sekt′ĕr), a line or plane that cuts a mathematical figure into two equal parts.

segment (seg′mənt), a section or division, a part marked off from another part.

intersection (in′tĕr sek′shən), point or line where one thing crosses another.

If we just say the "line AB," we mean a straight line *through* A and B, rather than a curved or zigzag path. We write this: $\overleftrightarrow{AB}$.

If we are thinking only of the *distance* from A to B, we speak of the "segment AB." We write this: $\overline{AB}$.

180

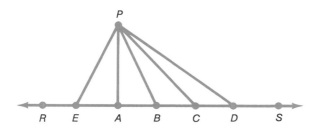

In order to tell how far it is from a point to a line, we use the segment which is the shortest distance, that is, the one which makes right angles with the line. Thus the distance from P to $\overleftrightarrow{RS}$ is $\overline{PA}$, because $\overline{PA}$ is shorter than $\overline{PB}$, $\overline{PC}$, $\overline{PD}$, or $\overline{PE}$.

> The shortest distance from a point to a line is always the perpendicular.

Now study this "kite" figure. Here line $\overleftrightarrow{PT}$ makes right angles with $\overline{AB}$ and passes through M, the midpoint of $\overline{AB}$.

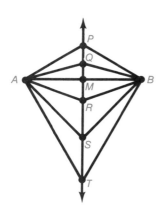

Would you agree that point P is just as far from point A as it is from point B?

Would you also agree that $\overline{QA} = \overline{QB}$, $\overline{RA} = \overline{RB}$, $\overline{SA} = \overline{SB}$, and $\overline{TA} = \overline{TB}$?

How does the distance $\overline{MA}$ compare with $\overline{MB}$?

We call line l the "perpendicular bisector" of $\overline{AB}$. We may conclude that:

> 1. Every point on the perpendicular bisector of a segment is equally distant from the ends of that segment.
> 2. Every point that is equally distant from the ends of a segment must lie on the perpendicular bisector of that segment.

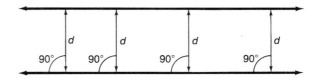

The distance between two parallel lines is the perpendicular distance between them. This is sensible, because we think of parallel lines as being equally far apart all along, like the rails of a railway track.

ACTIVITY

Copy these drawings onto your own paper and complete each task.

1. Where are all the points that are midway between two parallel lines, l and m? Show their location by drawing a dotted line.

2. Draw dotted lines to locate points that are the same distance (say *d* inches) from a given line *p*. (Remember that these points can be on either side of *p*.)

3. Use a dotted line to show the location of all the points that are equally distant from two cities, *R* and *S*.

4. You want to place a traffic light at the intersection of Broad and Main Streets so that it will be at the same distance from each of the four corners. Show by dotted lines where you would place the light.

5. Two towns are located at *A* and *B*; the railroad station is located at *S*. (a) Locate all the points that are just as far from *A* as they are from *S*. (b) Now locate all the points that are just as far from *B* as they are from *S*. (c) Can you find a point that is equally distant from *A*, *B*, and *S*?

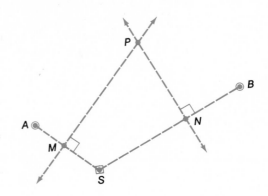

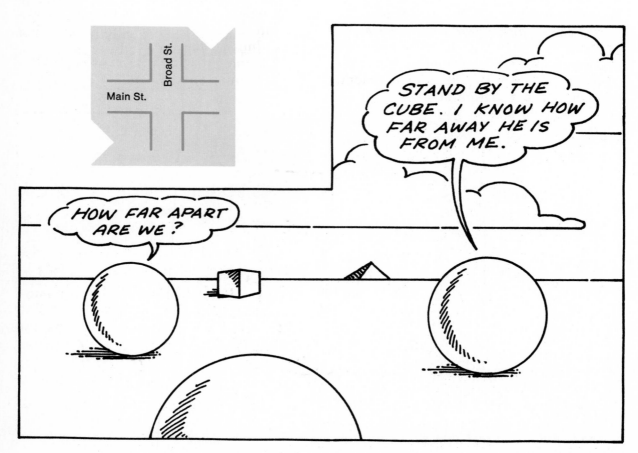

Working with Synonyms

Words that are similar in meaning are called *synonyms*. Number your paper 1 to 15. Find a synonym in the box for each underlined word in the story and write it on your paper.

smart	distinct	frantic
stoop	lucky	habit
strong	entertainment	condense
ask	endure	noteworthy
struggle	strange	respect

Last night I went to bed early, as is my usual (1) custom. I was nearly asleep when I heard an (2) unfamiliar sound outside my bedroom door. "Who's there?" I gasped.

But if the creature heard me (3) demand to know who was there, it did not answer.

Then, as (4) clear as could be, I heard my door creak open.

I was (5) clever enough to jump out of bed and (6) crouch down in a corner.

Whoever—whatever—was there crept closer. I wanted to (7) compress myself into a tiny ball and disappear. I felt that I couldn't (8) bear the fear another moment.

Something grabbed my neck. I made a (9) frenzied effort to break free. I'm a (10) sturdy person, but I couldn't get loose, (11) strive as I might. I only hoped I would be (12) fortunate enough to escape with my life!

Then the creature laughed, and I realized it was my sister. I felt a (13) remarkable surge of relief.

"Playing ghost?" I said coolly. "That's an interesting sort of (14) amusement. I (15) admire your cleverness."

"Weren't you scared?" she demanded.

"Of course not," I said.

Working With Antonyms _____

Words that are opposite in meaning are called *antonyms*. From the list in the box choose a word that is opposite in meaning to the underlined word. Write it on your paper. Continue writing the antonyms in order and number them.

relaxed	synonym	fiction
fail	solid	borrow
far	frigid	new
exact	silent	rear
bold	wrong	weak
joy	fresh	follow

This is the story of Antonym Ann
Who has a brother (1) _____ Sam
What Sam did right, Ann did (2) _____
When he was (3) _____ Ann was strong.
For Ann to succeed, Sam has to (4) _____;
When his bread is (5) _____, hers will be
    stale.
If Sam goes out the front door, Ann heads
    for the (6) _____.
When she travels (7) _____, he tries to
    stay near.
If Ann's story is (8) _____, Sam's will be
    fact;
Whenever she's vague, you know he's (9)
    _____.
Where Ann would lead, Sam would (10)
    _____.
If she says something is (11) _____, he
    says it's hollow.
Whenever Sam's timid, Ann is (12) _____.
When she wears a (13) _____ sweater, his
    must be old.
Sam likes torrid climates, and Ann likes it
    (14) _____;
When he's (15) _____, Ann knows she'll
    be rigid.
Whatever Sam will lend, Ann tries to (16)
    _____;
When he's full of (17) _____, she's bowed
    down by sorrow.
This was the story of Ann and Sam:
A talkative woman and a (18) _____ man.

184

Choosing the Right Definition _____

Sometimes a word has more than one meaning. When you look up a word in a dictionary, read all the definitions to find the one that best completes the meaning of the sentence you are reading.

Here are some words with three or more definitions. Complete the sentences that follow by choosing one of the words. Write it on your paper. After you have written the word, write next to it the number of the definition that best fits the meaning required in that particular sentence.

---

bond (1) That which binds; a band; tie. (2) Fetters; captivity. (3) An obligation or constraint. (4) An obligation in writing under a seal. (5) An interest-bearing certificate. (6) Bail, a surety.

cell (1) A small room, as for a prisoner. (2) A small cavity in the body. (3) A compartment of a storage battery. (4) The room occupied by a monk or nun. (5) A small unit of protoplasm of which living things are made.

flip (1) To snap off; hence, to toss carelessly. (2) To strike with a slight quick motion. (3) To flap, flounce about. (4) To snap jerkily.

press (1) A dense throng. (2) The act of crowding together. (3) Hurry or pressure of affairs. (4) A machine by which pressure is applied. (5) Newspapers or periodical literature collectively. (6) The art, process, or business of printing. (7) To push steadily against.

rapid (1) Having great speed. (2) Bearing the marks of or characterized by rapidity. (3) Done or completed in a short time. (4) A descent in a river less abrupt than a waterfall, usually in the plural, *rapids.*

rear (1) To lift up or raise. (2) To build up, erect. (3) To bring up, nurture, train.

---

1. **a.** Kim saw a small fish _____ about in the shallow water.
   b. Fred saw his father _____ a dead spider from the wall.

2. **a.** The prisoner was never allowed to go out of his _____.
   b. Last week we read about a simple animal that has just one _____.

3. **a.** I saw a filmstrip about how salmon _____ their young.
   b. As Jo looked at the stream she saw a huge turtle _____ its head.

4. **a.** In America we can say what we like in newspapers. We have freedom of the _____.
   b. She tried to _____ the elevator button.

5. **a.** Mr. Mason invested his son's money in a government _____.
   b. It was thought that John Irwin had stolen some money. He gave a _____ of $1,000 to keep from going to jail until his trial.

6. **a.** Mario went down the hill at a _____ pace.
   b. Salmon sometimes swim against swift _____ in rivers.

185

Finding Things in a Library

A. Finding the Right Drawer in a Card Catalog. The reference cards in a library are kept in drawers. All of the drawers together make up the card catalog. A library may have 60 or 70 drawers in the card catalog. Glance at the letters on the drawers in the same way that you glance at guide words in the dictionary until you find the one you want.

In one library the first seven drawers are lettered like this:

Drawer 1	Drawer 2	Drawer 3	Drawer 4	Drawer 5	Drawer 6	Drawer 7
A–ANA	ANB–ATO	ATR–BAY	BEA–BRA	BRE–CAL	CAM–CLO	CLU–DAI

On your paper, write the number of the drawer in which you would find each of the following:

1. Constitution of the United States
2. Canyons of the United States
3. Alexander Bell
4. A book by Louisa May Alcott
5. A book on California
6. *Arachne: The Skilled Weaver*
7. Marie Curie
8. Ralph Johnson Bunche

B. Reading Cards in the Card Catalog. As you probably know there are two, sometimes more, cards for each reference. The *title card* gives the name of the book first, and the *author card* gives the name of the author first. The title card is filed alphabetically according to the first main word in the title of the book. The author card is filed alphabetically according to the last name of the author. There is also a *subject card* for most books. Subject cards help you to find several books on one topic by different authors and with different titles.

Study the examples given here. Then write information as it would appear on a title card for each of these books. Use a separate sheet of paper.

1. *American Space Exploration*, by William Roy Shelton, published by Little, Brown & Co., Boston, 1967.

2. *The Mystery Began in Madeira*, by Mabel Allan, published by Criterion Books, New York, 1967.

3. *The African Season*, by Leonard Levitt, published by Simon & Schuster Inc., New York, 1967.

4. *Earth Treasures: Rocks and Minerals*, by Iris Tracy Comfort, published by Prentice-Hall, Inc., Englewood Cliffs, New Jersey, 1964.

Now write information as it would appear on an author card for each of the books. Use a separate sheet of paper.

970.1	This Land Was Theirs;
Osw	A Study of the North American Indian
	2d ed.
	Oswalt, Wendell H.
	Wiley, 1973
	617 p. illus. maps

Title Card

970.1	Oswalt, Wendell H.
Osw	
	This Land Was Theirs;
	A Study of the North American Indian
	2d ed.
	Wiley, 1973
	617 p. illus. maps

Author Card

970.1	Indians of North America
Osw	
	This Land Was Theirs;
	A Study of the North American Indian
2d ed	2d ed.
	Oswalt, Wendell H.
	Wiley, 1973
	617 p. illus. maps

Subject Card

Reviewing Prefixes and Suffixes _____

A. Among the suffixes that you have had, the ones that you meet most often are *ion* and *ation*. Both of these suffixes mean about the same thing: *act of, result of,* or *state of.* The suffix *ion* is nearly always pronounced as if it were spelled *shun.* The suffix *ation* is pronounced *ashƏn.*

On your paper add one of these suffixes to each word below to make a new word. If the word ends with *e*, drop the *e* before adding the suffix.

ion	ation

1. suggest
2. invent
3. evaporate
4. inform
5. generate
6. examine
7. celebrate
8. distribute
9. refrigerate

B. In the box below you will find prefixes you have had. On your paper write each word with the correct prefix to make the word mean the same thing as the phrase to the right of the word.

un	mis	out	under	over	trans	re	dis

1. state: to state again
2. common: not common
3. port: to carry across
4. courage: to lessen courage
5. reach: to reach too far
6. lead: to lead in a wrong direction
7. break: a breaking out
8. done: not done enough

C. On your paper add one of the suffixes in the box below to each of the words that follow. Be sure to add the suffix that will give the new word the same meaning as the phrase to the right of the word.

er	ist	ful	en	ly	less	ness	ment

1. regard: without regard
2. govern: the system by which a country is governed
3. steam: a boat run by the power of steam
4. state: the act of stating
5. wood: made of wood
6. help: full of help
7. improve: the act of being improved
8. sweet: the state or quality of being sweet
9. proud: with pride
10. alarm: one who alarms or warns, usually without reason

Working with Science Words

Many of the words below are in science textbooks. You should be able to pronounce these words correctly and understand their meaning.

Study the pronunciation of each of these words. Say the word to yourself, pronouncing it distinctly. Then read the meaning of the word and think about it.

astronomy (əs tron'ə mē), science dealing with the motions, positions, sizes and compositions of the stars, planets, and other heavenly bodies.

conservation (kon'sėr vā'shən), saving or replacing some natural resource for future use.

constellation (kon'stə lā'shən), a group of stars to which a name has been given.

eclipse (i klips'), passing from sight because light is cut off. Lunar eclipse—shutting out the light of the moon when the earth passes between it and the sun. Solar eclipse—shutting out the light of the sun when the moon passes between it and the earth.

electromagnet (i lek'trō mag'nit), a magnet in which magnetism has been produced by an electric current.

galaxy (gal'ək sē), a great island in space made up of millions of stars.

generator (jēn'ėr ā tėr), a machine which changes mechanical energy to electrical energy.

geologist (jē ol'ə jist), one who studies the physical history of the earth, layers of which the earth is composed, and the changes in the earth.

meteorologist (mē'tē ėr ol'ə jist), one who deals with the science of the atmosphere, particularly the weather and weather forecasting.

physicist (fiz'ə sist) one who studies mechanics, heat, light, sound, and electricity.

See if you know the meaning of these words as used in science. On your paper write the word that belongs in each blank space below. Add *s* if necessary.

1. A _____ is a group of stars, such as the Big Dipper.

2. The Milky Way is a great swarm of millions of stars. It is a _____.

3. _____ have discovered that light travels faster than sound.

4. Mr. Stevens used water only when it was necessary. He believed in water _____.

5. The local _____ predicted rain on the following day.

6. It is possible to make a magnet by passing electricity through a piece of iron. Such a magnet is called an _____.

7. If you should go into an electric power plant, you could see a _____ making electrical energy.

8. _____ have found that the earth's crust is composed of several different layers of rock.

9. When the moon shuts out the light by passing between the sun and the earth we are said to have a solar _____.

10. Some of the most recent discoveries in the field of _____ concern the composition of the moon.

9

Democracy Begins at Home

189

In the last story you read, the author gave you many hints about the theme, and even stated the theme near the end of the story. In the next story, it will be a little harder for you to decide on the theme. Before you start the story, read the first three questions in Activity 3. Think about these questions as you read. Remember the title will also give you a clue to the theme. When you have finished the story and know the answers to the questions, you should be able to state the theme in a single sentence.

Record your beginning and ending times.

What does it mean to you to be an American? In the next story, you will learn how being an American came to mean something very special to one boy.

That Special Feeling _____

Written for this book
by Juliana O. Muehrcke.

It had been a mistake to come to stay with the Delgados, Bobby Matthias thought. It was nice of the Delgados to let him stay with them while his parents were out of town. But Bobby just didn't fit in.

Now, for example, Mr. Delgado had called the family together for a meeting. Bobby couldn't think of a more boring way to spend the afternoon.

"Do I have to come?" Bobby grumbled.

"Sure," Victor Delgado told him. "While you're staying here, you're a member of the family. Come on."

Bobby followed, grumbling all the way. Family meetings! What a waste of time! He would never feel like a member of this odd-ball family.

Mr. and Mrs. Delgado were sitting at the kitchen table with Victor's sister Olga.

"I have the day off tomorrow," Mr. Delgado said, "and I thought we might all do something together. I suggest going to the band concert."

"Let's go horseback riding!" Olga cried.

"The ball game!" Victor chimed in.

"How about a picnic?" suggested Mrs. Delgado.

Mr. Delgado turned to Bobby, "What would you like to do, Bobby?"

"Me?" Bobby wasn't used to being asked his opinion. "Why don't you just decide?" he asked. "In my family, we don't have meetings."

"Some homes are run in a different way," said Mr. Delgado. "But in our home everyone has an equal chance to be heard and an equal vote."

Bobby squirmed in his chair.

"So what do you say?" Mr. Delgado asked him.

"Well," Bobby said hesitantly, "horseback riding sounds like fun. I've never done it."

They discussed the choices for a while, and then they voted. To Bobby's amazement, horseback riding was the winner.

190

"Good," said Mr. Delgado. "We'll get an early start for the stables."

"You mean we're really going?" Bobby found it hard to believe. *His* parents had never changed their plans because of a family vote.

"Majority rules in this family," Mr. Delgado said. "That's the principle America was founded on."

A warm feeling came over Bobby. His vote had really counted! It made him feel important. But Bobby wasn't good with words; so he didn't try to express the feeling.

The good feeling lasted until after dinner. And then it was suddenly shattered.

From his room, Bobby heard the doorbell ring, and a few minutes later Mr. Delgado called him. He clattered downstairs, still thinking about the horseback ride tomorrow. He could hardly wait.

Mr. Colby, the Delgados' neighbor, was standing in the doorway, holding a jacket over his arm.

"Hey, that looks like my jacket," Bobby said. And then he realized he'd said the wrong thing.

"I knew it!" Mr. Colby cried. "Some kids broke into my toolshed this morning. They stole some tools, broke some windows, and made a terrible mess. I didn't get a close look at them, but I recognized Bobby's jacket. I've seen him wearing it enough times. And when they ran, Bobby left his jacket behind."

Bobby's heart sank. He had been in trouble before, and he was afraid of what would happen next. But Mr. Delgado asked gently, "Did you do it, Bobby?"

"No," Bobby said.

"But I caught him red-handed!" Mr. Colby said.

"What do you mean, red-handed," said

Mr. Delgado. "You only saw his jacket. In America a person is innocent till proven guilty. Bobby says he didn't do it, and I believe him. So the question is, How did his jacket get there? When did you see your jacket last, Bobby?"

Bobby opened his mouth and closed it again. He knew that if he said he had lost his jacket it would sound like a lie, even though it was the truth. So he just mumbled, "I can't remember."

"A likely story!" scoffed Mr. Colby. "He's guilty, and I want him to pay for it!"

There goes my allowance for the next year, Bobby thought. And there goes the horseback ride tomorrow. Mr. Delgado surely wouldn't let him go now.

"Wait a minute," Victor said. "Lots of people have jackets like that. How do you know it's Bobby's?"

"A good question," said Mr. Delgado. "Bobby, try on the jacket." Bobby tried to put the jacket on, but it was far too small.

Mr. Colby frowned. "I guess I jumped to conclusions," he said sheepishly.

"It's lucky we live in a democracy, isn't it?" said Mr. Delgado. "In a dictatorship, Bobby could have been condemned without a fair trial."

"Sorry," mumbled Mr. Colby, backing out the door.

Again Bobby felt that special glow. This time he did put it into words.

"It may sound corny," he said, "but I'm proud to be an American."

1 ACTIVITY

Fact Questions

Answer the following questions on a separate sheet of paper.

1. Why was Bobby staying with the Delgados?

2. What was the purpose of the family meeting?

3. What was decided at the family meeting?

4. What was Mr. Colby carrying when he rang the Delgados' doorbell?

5. Why did Mr. Colby think that Bobby had broken into his tool shed?

6. What had really happened to Bobby's jacket?

7. Why didn't Bobby say that he had lost the jacket?

8. When Mr. Colby accused him, what did Bobby expect Mr. Delgado to do?

9. How did Bobby prove his innocence?

10. Why did Bobby have a warm feeling at the end of the story?

Copy this chart on your paper. Compute and record your WPM as you did on page 28.

Give yourself a score of 10 for each correct answer in Activity 1. This is your comprehension score. Record it on the chart.

	Hr.	Min.	Sec.
Ending Time:	___	___	___
Beginning time:	___	___	___
Total Time:	___	___	___

No. words:
No. seconds: $\left(\dfrac{785}{}\right) \times 60 = $ _____ **WPM**

Comprehension score: _____

2 ACTIVITY — Thought Questions

On your own paper, write the answers to these questions.

1. Did Bobby feel and act like a member of the family at the beginning of the story? How can you tell?

2. Name two rights that a person has in a democracy that do not exist in a dictatorship.

3. Do you think the idea of family meetings is good or bad? Why?

3 ACTIVITY — Thinking About Theme

Think over the story you just read. Then answer the following questions. Use your own paper.

1. To what form of government would you compare the Delgado family's way of life?

2. Give two examples to prove your answer to question #1.

3. Why do the ideals of democracy mean more to Bobby at the end of the story than at the beginning?

4. What is the theme of this story?

**HOW TO READ IN
SOCIAL STUDIES**

Making a summary paragraph of main ideas after you read will often prove useful to you. You can use such a summary to refresh your memory on main points when giving a report. If you save several of these summaries you will find them very helpful to use for review when you are studying for a test.

If the subject you are reading about could have any effect on your own life, try to reason out what that effect is. Thinking of the effect which any event in history has on your own life is the best way of making your reading of social studies material interesting, meaningful, and vivid.

1. Read the selection carefully and notice the sentence that gives the main idea in each paragraph.
2. Do Activity 1.

In the story you have just read, Mr. Delgado believed that democracy begins at home.

What are the advantages of democracy that all of us enjoy, often without thinking much about them? Some of these advantages will be discussed in the next selection. Read to find out what they are.

The Advantages of Democracy —

Written for this book
by Enid Johnson

On May 27, 1787, a convention was opened in Philadelphia to consider the problems of the newly formed American government. During the convention our Constitution was drafted. Later, the Bill of Rights was added. The original Constitution, together with the Bill of Rights, paved the way for democracy to become our form of government. Today we enjoy many advantages as a result of the work of our ancestors who planned our present form of government.

One advantage of our democracy is that it was designed to insure equal opportunity for all. Equal opportunity means that all citizens should be free to choose the work they want to do, to earn as much as they are capable of earning, and to invest their savings in any way they like. Workers have the right to belong to unions and to strike with their group for higher wages if the group thinks it should have more pay. In some countries the people have none of these rights. They have to do the kind of work the government wants them to do, and the government sets the amount of pay it thinks workers should have.

---

advantage (ad van′tij), anything that is to the good, or is a benefit.

convention (kən ven′shən), a meeting arranged for a particular purpose.

draft (draft), to write out a plan or rough copy of.

privilege (priv′l ij), a right granted as a favor.

dictator (dik′tā tẽr), a person having complete power and authority.

194

Another privilege of people who live in a democracy is the right to take part in the affairs of government. Every person of legal age who is properly registered has the right to vote. We may choose the person we want to represent us from several people who are running for office. The governing bodies of the states and of the federal government are made up of men and women chosen by the people. If we want a certain law passed, we have the right to send a message to the people who are representing us at the state or national capital. We have the right to tell them what we would like them to do.

A third advantage is our freedom of religious worship. Each of us may attend any church we like. The government does not interfere in any way with our religious beliefs or how we express them. In some countries the government encourages the people to attend one church. In others, the government discourages its people from going to church or having any religious belief at all. Even to this day it is common in some countries for religious leaders to be jailed or punished.

Freedom to have a jury trial is an additional privilege which our democracy offers. A person is believed innocent until judged guilty by a jury of equals. Everyone is entitled to a fair trial. How different is this system from that in countries in which a person may be thrown into prison or killed if a dictator so orders.

A fifth advantage is freedom of speech. We are free to talk about the affairs of our government, to discuss its problems, and to say how we think they should be solved. (This privilege, of course, is not given to those who want to overthrow our democratic form of government by force.) In some countries anyone who dares to say that anything is wrong with the government or to make a suggestion for its improvement is punished.

Finally, we enjoy freedom of the press. In many countries the government controls all the newspapers and magazines. Only that information which the government wants them to have can be given to the people. Our papers and magazines are free to give any available information to our people, so long as it is founded on facts and does not endanger the security of our country. Our press is also free to criticize people in public office and the things that they do.

These are but a few of the advantages of our democracy. As a free nation, we should be able to make the most of our resources, our energies, and our abilities.

1 ACTIVITY Writing a Summary

Combine the main ideas of each paragraph to make a summary. Write the summary, making sure that all the main ideas are included. Don't just copy sentences from the book. Write the summary in your own words. Use a separate sheet of paper.

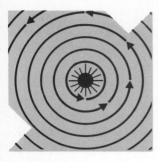

HOW TO READ IN SCIENCE

You know that in reading science material it is important to read carefully and pay attention to details. Sometimes there are many details to remember. To help you remember the details in a science article, it is a good idea to take notes. As you read, write down the main idea and the important details in each paragraph. You don't have to write in complete sentences, or make a formal outline, so you can use very few words.

Note taking is one of the most important study skills. Try taking notes on the main ideas and details as you read this short science article. Then use your notes to answer the Fact Questions in Activity 1 without looking back at the article. Even if you have to look back, your notes will help you know where in the article to find the information you need. You will not have to search through the entire article.

(*Hint:* it may help to look at the questions first.)

Every freedom brings with it a responsibility. Read the following article to learn more about the responsibility we all have to the world we live in.

Freedom and Responsibility

Written for this book
by Leonard Bernstein.

Most people use the word democratic to mean free—a democracy is a "free country." Indeed, the liberties guaranteed to us by the Constitution are essential to a democratic society. But no society can be totally free. Individuals must often limit their freedom for the good of society as a whole. Laws set limits, but laws cannot govern every aspect of human behavior. This is why, if we examine the ideals of democracy carefully, we can find another important thread that weaves its way through the Constitution and through the history of the United States. It is a thread that binds people to one another and to their country—the thread of responsibility.

Responsibility is a very complex word. It can be used in many ways. Unfortunately, people have used the word in a very limited way, perhaps even in a selfish way. We usually think of responsibility in terms of what we should do for ourselves, our families, and our friends. But this is not where it ends. Responsibility, in a broader sense, means thinking about all our actions, and about the effects those actions will have on ourselves, on other people, and on the world we live in. In this sense, the word responsibility can apply to every aspect of life.

For more than thirty years, people have been examining a serious question of re-

---

extinction (ik stiŋk′ shən), the state of going out of existence.

sponsibility. One of the results of this examination has been the development of a new branch of science: *ecology*. Ecology concerns itself with the interrelationships of living things and their environment. Ecologists have found that people, in order to meet their needs, have used their invented ways to alter the environment. In doing so, they have behaved in an irresponsible way, misusing and abusing the earth's resources to a point of danger. The warning signs are all around us. Some of the more outstanding ones are pollution, shortage of energy, and even extinction of certain animal species.

Why is the environment so important, and why is it so urgent that we begin to treat our natural resources responsibly?

In 1809, the French scientist Lamarck introduced a new word into the field of science. The word is *biosphere*, which means the total area of our planet which is able to support life. Compared with the size of the earth and its surrounding at-mosphere, the biosphere is a very small area. As a matter of fact, it is only about thirteen miles (21 kilometers) thick, with some life being found seven miles (11 kilometers) deep in the ocean, and some six miles (9.6 kilometers) up in the mountains. And most life is found in only a very narrow region within the biosphere. Most types of plants and animals are restricted to the available space within this narrow region. It may seem hard to believe that ninety percent of the ocean and thirty percent of the land contain almost no life at all! With so many living things in such a small area, available living space is very precious. If we destroy any more of the biosphere, making it unfit for supporting life, the results will be disastrous.

Conserving natural resources may involve limiting our freedom to some extent. But then, knowing when to set limits on freedom, and doing it for the good of all, is the meaning of responsibility. In this case, our lives may depend on it.

ACTIVITY 1 — Fact Questions

1. According to this article, what is the broad meaning of the word, *responsibility*?

2. With what is the science of ecology concerned?

3. What are three signs that we have treated our environment in an irresponsible way?

4. What is the biosphere?

5. What percent of the ocean does not contain life?

6. What percent of the land does not support life?

ACTIVITY 2 — Thought Questions

1. Why can't any society be totally free, without limits or restrictions?

2. What would be some of the "disastrous" results if any of the biosphere becomes incapable of supporting life?

3. What are a few ways in which individual people might have to limit their freedom for the good of the environment?

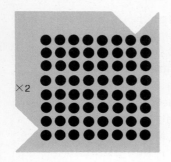

HOW TO READ IN MATHEMATICS

As you work with this mathematics lesson, you will be reading diagrams, numerals, and words in sentences, as well as some money values. As you read, think carefully so that you will grasp the important ideas about the growth of numbers.

Under our democratic form of government the United States has grown rapidly in different ways, and it is still growing. It has grown in the number of states that it contains. It has grown in population. The income of our country grows each year. In this lesson you will learn some of the ways in which numbers may grow mathematically.

Ways in Which Numbers Grow —

Written for this book
by William L. Schaaf.

Let us see some of the ways in which numbers might "grow." Consider the numbers from 1 to 10 inclusive. What is their sum? Here is an easy way to find the sum without actually adding. Notice that the pairs from each end always add to 11, as shown by the brackets.

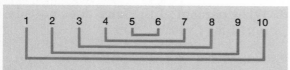

Notice also that the number of pairs is half of 10, or 5. So, the sum is 5×11, or 55. Prove this result by actually adding all the numbers from 1 to 10 inclusive.

We can use the same scheme even when the numbers differ by 2 rather than by 1. Consider the first ten *odd* numbers:

Would you agree that their sum is

$$5 \times (1 + 19) = 5 \times 20 = 100?$$

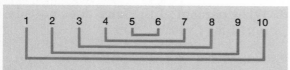

inclusive (in klōo′ siv), including everything concerned.

1

ACTIVITY

Use your own paper to write the answers to these questions.

1. Without adding them directly, find the sum of the first 26 numbers from 1 to 26 inclusive:

$$\{1,2,3,4, \ldots 23,24,25,26\}$$

2. Find the sum of the first 12 even numbers:

$$\{2,4,6, \ldots 20,22,24\}$$

3. Find the sum of all the whole numbers from 21 to 30 inclusive.

4. Find the sum of the following set of numbers:

$$\{5,10,15,20, \ldots 50,55,60\}$$

198

5. What is the sum of all the whole numbers from 1 to 100 inclusive?

6. Try to find the sum of this set of whole numbers:
$$\{1,2,3,4,5,6,7,8,9,10,11\}$$

7. Can you see what to do when adding an *odd* number of numbers?

Series That Grow by Multiplying

In all the series we have talked about so far, each number after the first was obtained by *adding* the same number to each in order to get the next number.

Now let us look at some series in which each number is obtained by *multiplying* by the same number to get the next number. For example: 1, 2, 4, 8, 16, 32, etc.

Here each number is twice as large as the one just before it—we have multiplied each number by 2 to get the next number. Can you see that such a series might "grow" quite rapidly?

ACTIVITY 2

Answer each question on your own paper.

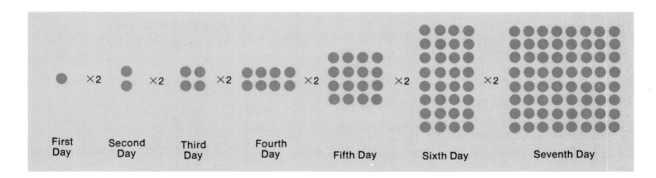

First Day Second Day Third Day Fourth Day Fifth Day Sixth Day Seventh Day

1. Suppose you put a penny away in a toy bank today, 2¢ tomorrow, 4¢ the next day, then 8¢, and so on for one week (7 days).

   a. How much would you have to put in the bank on the seventh day?

   b. How much would you have in the bank altogether?

2. If you kept this up for 1 month, you would have to put $10,737,418.24 into the bank on the last day of the month! How much would you have to put in the bank on the *next to the last day of the month?* (You might be interested to know that the total amount in the bank at the end of 31 days would be $21,474,-836.47.)

Taking Notes on an Encyclopedia Article _____

Suppose that your teacher suggested that you look up *bamboo* in an encyclopedia and prepare to give a report to the class.

Below is an article on bamboo which appears in an encyclopedia. Read it and take notes which you might use in making an oral report.

First, glance through the article to find with what topic each paragraph deals. Write the topic of each paragraph on your paper, leaving plenty of space under each topic for major details. Number each topic with a Roman numeral. Use capital letters for the details.

Next read the details in each paragraph. Jot these details down under the topic of the paragraph. Use just as few words as possible—only enough to remind you of the information when you want to tell it to others.

At the end of the article, notes have been made on the first paragraph. Copy these notes onto your own paper. Change the wording if you think of a better wording. Then continue taking notes on the rest of the article.

Bamboo. One of the most valuable and widespread plants is bamboo. It is a tall, treelike grass. Nearly 500 species grow in Asia, in North and South America, and in Africa. It is a tropical plant, but it will grow in temperate zones. Asiatic varieties have been brought into the United States and Europe.

A single root may produce as many as 100 stems. They are polished and jointed. The hollow stems are sometimes three feet (0.9 meter) around. Young sprouts grow fast, at times a foot (30 centimeters) or more a day. They may rise 30, 50, or even 120 feet (9, 15, 36 meters). Near the top are many branches. Some species produce flowers and seeds yearly. Others do not bloom for 60 years or more.

Bamboo products range from food to houses. Oriental cooks serve peeled sprouts as vegetables. They also candy and pickle them. Americans import canned bamboo shoots for chop suey. In the Far East, people use the hollow stems for water pipes and for building bridges and houses. Short sections serve as pails and cooking utensils. Split into strips, the stems make planks for walls, floors, and roofs. Thinner strips are woven into mats, chairs, cages, and curtains. Bamboo fishing rods are made of matched strips glued together. Split bamboo is also used for chopsticks and fan ribs. The inner parts of the stem are made into quality papers.[3]

Suggested Notes on the First Paragraph

Bamboo

1. Tall treelike grass; valuable.

  A. 500 species

  B. Grows in Africa, Asia, and in the Americas

HOW DO YOU SPELL BAMBOO?

Making Generalizations

Many paragraphs contain a series of related facts about one subject. Sometimes you need to remember each of these separate facts. At other times all you need to do is to get a general idea of what the several facts imply when taken together. The general conclusion you draw from several facts is called a *generalization.*

See if you can make a generalization after reading the facts in each of these paragraphs. The first generalization has been written for you. Write the others on your own paper.

1. Perhaps you think pilots and cabin attendants are the only types of workers employed by an airline. If you were to visit an airport you would see ticket agents, secretaries, typists, and book-keepers—all at work on the airline's business. There are the highly skilled mechanics who keep the planes in good flying condition. Cargo handlers take care of the mailbags, express, and baggage. A superintendent works with the pilot of each plane to plan the route and altitude. Air traffic controllers direct takeoffs and landings.

   What generalization can you make about the employees of an airline?

   Many different workers are employed by an airline.

2. New England has no iron or coal mines, no oil wells, and no natural gas. Because glaciers pushed away the rich topsoil, the soil is poor in most places. In many places only bare rocks were left after the glaciers passed over the land.

   What is your generalization concerning the natural resources and the prosperity of New England?

3. In oceans there are many kinds of large animals such as whales and porpoises. Snails, clams, lobsters, crabs, and eels also live in the sea. These animals are large enough so that a person can see them with the naked eye. But there are also billions of animals in the sea that cannot be seen without a microscope.

   What generalization would you make about animals that live in the sea?

4. Some seeds are scattered by the wind. For example, the white head of the dandelion is made up of seeds with a parachute attached to each one. Some seeds have wings which help them to "fly" through the air. Seeds of the maple, ash, thistle, and milkweed have wings. Water also helps to scatter seeds. The seeds of grass, the sycamore, and the bitter pecan are light enough to float in water. Some plans scatter their own seeds. When their seed pods are ripe, they burst open with such force that their seeds are scattered for quite a distance.

   What generalization can you make in regard to the ways in which seeds travel?

201

Using an Encyclopedia Index

Most encyclopedias have indexes. The index can give you some information even before you read the articles on your subject. The list of items under each main topic gives you a brief summary of the information in the topic.

The chief value of the index, however, is to tell you where to look if you wish to find all of the information which the complete set of volumes has to give about a topic or one aspect of a topic.

If you had to write a paper on Benjamin Franklin, it wouldn't be enough just to read about Franklin in Volume F. Turning to the index you would find references to many pages in many different volumes where you would find information in addition to that given in the F volume. These additional references are called *cross references*.

In some encyclopedias, the index uses the *letter* of the volume in given cross references, as C-9. In others, the number of the volume is used, as 3-9. When the number of a volume is used, it often appears in boldface type.

Study the entries that follow and answer the questions. Use your own paper.

Index[4]

Franklin, Benjamin (1706–90), American scientist, inventor, and statesman: F-422–8, A-345–6, *pictures* F-422, 424, 426–8, *color picture* P-180
Albany Congress R-162–3, A-243, N-249
American tall tales F-295, *picture* F-295
'Autobiography' A-345
autograph, *pictures* A-745, D-55
benevolent trusts F-361
birthday begins Thrift Week F-92
Constitutional Convention F-428
daylight saving D-41
Declaration of Independence D-51, *pictures* D-50, A-17, R-162: signature reproduced D-55
diplomatic service F-426–7, *pictures* F-426–7
early American magazine M-35
grave, *map* P-251b
Gulf Stream charted and named by G-259b
Hall of Fame, *table* H-11
inventor and scientist F-425–6
  bifocal lenses S-370, *picture* I-248
  fireplace S-483, *picture* A-334
  fluid theory of electricity E-139

harmonica H-34
lightning experiments F-425, E-153, *picture* F-426
stove S-483, F-425, *picture* I-297b
telegraphy experiments T-54
Lord Howe and, *picture* R-174
painting by Benjamin West, *picture* W-100
persuades Pulaski to aid colonists P-531
'Poor Richard's Almanack' F-424, R-131, *pictures* F-425, R-130
portrait, *pictures* F-428, B-163: bust by Houdon, S-88, *picture* S-88; on first stamps, *pictures* P-439, S-408; on $100 bill, *table* M-429
postal service F-424–5, P-460 c-d
Saunders, Richard, pen name F-424
Stamp Act, F-426, S-409; repeal, *picture* F-427
subscription library L-215
time line F-423
toleration of opinions C-552
treaty of peace with England R-173, 174

Longfellow, Henry Wadsworth (1807–82), American poet L-346–8, A-364, *picture* L-346, *color picture* M-62
autograph, *picture* A-745

books by L-348
bust in Westminster Abbey, *picture* L-342
Cambridge home C-56b, L-347, 348, *picture* L-347
'Courtship of Miles Standish, The' L-348, S-410, *picture* A-349
'Evangeline' A-8
Hall of Fame, *table* H-11
place in American literature A-350
'Santa Filomena', poem N-289
'Song of Hiawatha, The' H-150, L-348, M-274: quotation from W-92
statue, *color picture* M-60
translated 'Frithjof's Saga' S-526
Wayside Inn, *picture* L-346

Mars, a planet P-352–3, 350, *pictures* P-353
atmosphere P-353
ice cap P-353, *pictures* P-353
Kepler studies motions K-46
name M-118
planets compared, *table* P-351
position in aerospace, *color diagram* A-47
probes P-352, 353, S-344, *diagram* S-343b
red appearance P-353
satellites (moons) S-52
sun, relation to, *diagram* P-352, *table* P-351

1. What did Franklin work on as an inventor and scientist?

2. Where would you find information about
   a. bifocal lenses?
   b. *Poor Richard's Almanack?*

3. Where would you find information about
   a. Longfellow's home?
   b. Longfellow's *Hiawatha?*

4. When did Longfellow live?

5. Where would you look in order to find
   a. a diagram of Mars' position?
   b. the origin of the name of this planet?
   c. a comparison of other planets to Mars?

Critical Reading: Faulty Reasoning

We all use reasoning to convince others to come around to our point of view, or to help them understand something. Reasoning is a valuable part of communication when it reflects clear and logical thinking. However, there are pitfalls that a person can easily fall into. One of the most common is the hasty generalization. A hasty generalization means jumping to a conclusion without enough evidence.

You have learned a lot of what you know about the world by making generalizations. That is, you collected a number of instances or examples and drew a conclusion from them. Suppose, for example, that you don't know that black jelly beans are licorice flavored. You try one, and it tastes like licorice. You try another one with the same result. After sampling a few more, you can be pretty sure, although not certain, that black jelly beans are licorice flavored. The more sampling you do, the more sure you will be. The conclusion you draw from enough evidence is likely to be a sound generalization.

However, when you jump to a conclusion without enough evidence, you fall into the error of making a hasty generalization. Suppose, for example, that you are visiting a strange city and notice several people tossing candy bar wrappers or other bits of paper onto the sidewalks. On your way home, you comment on what litterbugs the people of that city are. Your conclusion may be accurate, but you can't be sure because you have seen only a few instances. There may be many more people in that city who don't litter than those who do. To draw a sound generalization about the habits of a large number of people, careful observation over a long period of time would be required.

When you make a generalization, consider the amount of evidence you have to go on. In your reading, be sure to test the generalizations that other people make.

Study each of the following statements. On your paper write whether you think each is probably a sound generalization or probably a hasty one. Briefly, give your reason for your decision.

1. A high-school-age driver backed into our car at the shopping center last week. Just today, I read about an accident involving a teen-age driver. Obviously, teen-age drivers are likely to have accidents.

2. An overpass was built last year because so many residents of the Winterset section were walking across a dangerous railroad track. A survey shows that, after six months, eight out of ten residents are still dodging trains instead of using the overpass. I guess it's hard to get these people to put safety above convenience.

3. I noticed three Cadillacs outside the Franklin Junior High School the other night while the PTA meeting was going on. I guess mostly rich kids go there.

NOW DON'T JUMP TO ANY CONCLUSIONS.